Leach Pottery St Ives

The Legacy of Bernard Leach

Marion Whybrow

Bernard Leach and his cohorts

First Published in hardback and paperback 2006
Beach Books, St Ives, Cornwall

ISBN 0 9522461 4 7

Design - Kim Lynch, Riverside, Lelant, Cornwall

Printed and bound in Singapore
by Imago

Colleagues whose enthusiasm and commitment was vital in the making of this book

John Bedding Potter. Trained at Leach Pottery. Works at Gaolyard Studios, Dove Street, St Ives. Owns St Ives Ceramics, Fish Street, specialising in Leach influenced potters and world-wide pottery. Trustee of Bernard Leach (St Ives) Trust Ltd.

Jon Grimble As well as collecting art, is proprietor of Porthminster Gallery, Fernlea Terrace, St Ives, specialising in post-war St Ives and Newlyn abstract art, pottery and sculpture, including Terry Frost and Sandra Blow.

Denny Long Trained as a potter but is now a print maker and mixed media artist. She gained an MA from Falmouth School of Art in Installation. She is a recently elected Academician of the Royal West of England Academy and Associate of the Newlyn Society of Artists.

Trixie Lucas University lecturer before becoming a stockbroker in Johannesburg and London. Now married, with a family. She and her husband Fred, are keen collectors of paintings, sculpture and pottery.

Roger Tonkinson Architect, art collector. Owner of Tremayne Applied Arts, Street-an-Pol, St Ives, specialising in Arts & Crafts, Art Nouveau and 20th century designer furniture, pottery and artifacts.

Kim Lynch Designer. Trained at Harrow College of Art. With husband, Joseph, owns Waterside Gallery, Street-an-Pol, St Ives. Specialising in seascape/landscape and figurative paintings, pottery and sculpture.

Marion Whybrow Has written extensively on the St Ives Arts Colony, its painters, potters and sculptors, past and present. (see page 232) Married to painter Terry Whybrow.

Bernard Leach 1887-1979

Contents

Drawing of Bernard Leach by Hyman Segal

*Bernard Leach, a towering figure in the world of ceramics,
was more than a craftsman potter. He was a leader;
a teacher of aesthetics and excellence,
from whom generations of potters took their
inspiration and example.
This book pays tribute to Leach's dynamic influence
and provides testimony, not only in words,
but in portraying the many excellent craftsmen and women
who have become masters of their craft.
In doing this they pay tribute to their working time
at the Leach Pottery and in particular to their contact with
Bernard Leach and his philosophy.*

Marion Whybrow

Foreword

John Bedding

Over the years there has been much written on the life and works of Bernard Leach, but very little if any on his workshop in St Ives. This was why Marion's first book 'The Leach Legacy' was such a valuable addition to the story. It told the story in part, of the pottery through the students that worked there and what they have achieved since. The strength of Bernard Leach's influence is in the students he trained and the belief he instilled. It was not only a professional training, but also a philosophy and culture and through his students his influence expanded worldwide.

The Leach Pottery is at the moment on the cusp of a new chapter in its history. Roger Tonkinson, Denny Long, Jon Grimble, myself and Trixie Lucas, persuaded Marion to republish, update and expand her original book. We felt the material was too valuable to be lost, its relevance even more important in the light of events. She made renewed contacts with the former students and was met with a wave of enthusiasm that surprised us all. I was asked to add a chapter on the daily life and workings of the workshop from a personal perspective. Writing it gave me pangs of nostalgia and I was surprised at the memories that came flooding back. The result is only a brief glimpse into the rich and colourful life of the Leach Pottery.

Leach Pottery Workshop 1968 – 1978

I arrived at the Leach Pottery in 1968 at the age of 21 from a background in small commercial and designer potteries in London and St Ives. For the first time I encountered real flames in the kilns and a strong philosophical attitude to the making and looking at pots and like many before and after me it changed my life and my attitude towards pottery forever.

The students and staff

I had been working for Troika pottery a local St Ives pottery, when I got the call from Janet Leach to say she had a vacancy. We were called 'student apprentices,' we came from differing backgrounds, countries, and levels of experiences, but all with one aim: to learn from the master potter, Bernard Leach. Our primary task was to make the Leach standard-ware, which was a range of domestic pottery originally designed by Bernard and his son David, but over the years it had evolved and been perfected through the hands of the main thrower William (Bill) Marshall.

Trevor and myself firing the single chamber oil kiln, with Bill Marshall giving advice

Our apprenticeship period was for two years, after which it was hoped we had gained enough experience to start up our own workshops. As most students had already been at least to college, it was a good postgraduate bridge into the professional world. There were however exceptions to the rule, some came with little or no experience while others had already owned and run their own workshops.

When I arrived Trevor Corser had just moved up after many years of being a part-time packer and clay-man, to be taken on as a student. He occupied a wheel opposite mine and was to become a lifelong friend. Trevor was also to become the longest serving member of the pottery, seeing it through some of the most difficult times in its long history. Another virtual novice in 1968 was Harry Isaacs. He had come to work in the pottery the previous summer employed as a general helper, and came from a background in the music industry. Janet had invited him to work on a wheel and train as a potter. His secondary job when I arrived was packing and firing the main oil kiln along with Ian Steele, an experienced potter. Harry left the pottery the following year and although teaching pottery at local night classes for many years never became a professional potter. He did however in 2004 become Town Mayor an anecdote we would love to have shared around the fireplace had we the benefit of precognition.

With this variable mix of experience Janet Leach became concerned about the lack of continuity in the standards of the ware. This was a constant flaw in the system, the students made the production-ware, but when there were several new arrivals they had to be trained up to learn the shapes and gain proficiency in making them. There were seven wheels and Bill Marshall was the only experienced staff potter making the standard-ware. If two or more wheels were occupied by new arrivals it was natural that the standards and output went down. Janet decided that she should employ another staff potter with experience. She brought in Alan Brough; he had previously been running his own pottery in Brixham, Devon and added much needed experience to the group. I also was to become a member of the staff, as too was Trevor Corser. I became a staff member in 1972. I had completed my two years in 1970 and went to work in a French work-shop for a year. When I returned Janet was still concerned with the lack of continuity in the workshop, as Alan Brough was leaving. She asked me to join the staff and I gratefully accepted as I had so much enjoyed my previous time there and felt I still had a lot to learn.

Michael Cardew, Bill Marshall and Bernard on a Leach Pottery outing to Michael Cardew's pottery at Wenford Bridge

An influential and interesting arrival in 1969 was the Japanese potter Shigeyoshi Ichino. He came from a traditional pottery in the ancient Tamba district of Japan, where there were pottery traditions dating back over 700 years. Janet Leach had worked there under Shigey's father, Tanso, before she married Bernard. Janet had promised Tanso that she would bring his eldest son Shigey to England to study English pottery. When he arrived Shigey had very little English, but was a very experienced and accomplished potter and an excellent thrower. He brought over with him his traditional style kick wheel. This was a beautifully made momentum wheel with a short base-axel and low weighted flywheel which made it impossible for Westerners to use, but which I had to master when I later worked in Japan.

We all learnt a lot from Shigey, from his mastery at making a variety of delicately made bamboo tools to the Japanese style of throwing off a mound of clay, instead as we do, weigh up balls of clay to throw from. His biggest contribution though, was to revitalise the use of the climbing kiln. Before I arrived a large single chamber oil kiln had been built. This had a faster firing cycle than the climbing kiln and it needed fewer pots to fill; it also needed less labour in firing and it had become seductive to use this exclusively.

The chambered kiln, which was oil and wood fired, had become virtually redundant. With the arrival of Shigey and his wood firing experience and a general feeling that the climbing kiln was the true spirit of the pottery, it was again put into service. There was nothing like firing that kiln, for me it was a totally new experience; flames billowed from every crevice and gave a gut feeling of truly battling with the elements. It also changed the atmosphere in the workshop; there was a celebratory feeling after every firing, which had the effect of bonding the group as a team.

Kiln supper. Left to right: Terry Brunyee, Janet Leach, Sylvia Hardaker, Lynne Isaacs

Apart from the seven of us making the standard-ware, there were others making up the staff. Mary Yates was the secretary at the time; she also served occasionally in the showroom, although in the summer a showroom assistant was employed. Dave Sturt and later Bob Dagnall were the general help, their duties were to mix clay, pack pots for shipping, and other chores such as gardening. Judi Gardner glazed pots, packed the biscuit kiln, made the few moulded pots produced, and helped Janet with her pots.

Janet Leach worked in her own studio under her flat in the cottage. She made exclusively her own pots and although she put some pots into the standard kiln she had her own kiln, as she liked control over the firing of her pots. Her firings went long into the early morning and either Trevor or I would fire the kiln, with Janet on our shoulder.

She particularly liked to prepare a kiln supper for everyone, at which time the kiln would be slowed down while we ate. Once kilns are put into reverse they take a long time to regain momentum and climb in temperature again. Her kiln was also prone to carbon build up in the fire-mouth. This formed as a rose, or obstruction, which had to be removed, usually in the early hours of the morning at white heat temperatures. The kiln had to be turned off and the rose dug out, while the person extracting it would be frying in the heat. Then came the laborious task of regaining temperature with a very inefficient kiln. Years later Trevor and I redesigned and rebuilt the fire-mouth, which made the task of firing it a less trying experience.

Bernard also only made his own work and came to the pottery in the afternoons. He would arrive about 2pm; sometimes wander around for a chat, before disappearing upstairs to his studio above the clay-room. He would reappear at crib-time (afternoon tea), sit beside the fireplace and hold court as we surrounded him on stools. Subjects would vary from the topical and light, to heavier philosophical ponderings of the world, religion and pots. He would then disappear again into his studio until about 5pm when a taxi would come to take him back to his flat at Barnaloft on Porthmeor Beach.

The fireplace where we gathered at crib-time. Just off centre is the iron kettle that Bernard always sat on

Sometimes Bill Marshall would accompany him in his studio to help him make the larger pots. At this time Bernard was around 83 years of age and still using a kick wheel, although not frail he did not really have the strength to throw large balls of clay. Also his eyesight was deteriorating, a condition that would later keep him from making altogether. When I returned from France he no longer worked in his studio, but spent most of his time in Barnaloft writing his final book 'Beyond East and West.'

Relationships with Bernard

As anyone that has seen pictures of Bernard in his workshop will notice, he always worked in a shirt and tie and wore polished brogues on his feet. He was every bit the gentleman potter, but in no way was he stiff and unapproachable as might be suspected. His relationships with his students were friendly and paternal. With the gap in experience, accomplishments, and reputation, I found it difficult at first not to be intimidated, but with the relaxed and non-hierarchal atmosphere in the pottery I did come to regard Bernard as a father figure and dare I say it Janet as 'mother.'

One of Bernard's tasks before disappearing into his studio in the afternoons was to visit our wheels and check the quality of the day's work, especially if you were a new student. One of my early experiences of Bernard's humour and quick thinking was of a time when he was on one of these missions. He was standing by my wheel looking at my pots, when he leant on a full board, which tipped over. The pots fell to the floor in a patter; Bernard gave me a slight smile and said, "Well Johnnie I was going to tell you to smash those," and walked off with a big grin on his face.

Another task that Bernard performed was the pricing and selecting of individual pots for the showroom. We all worked an eight to five day making standard-ware. In the evenings and weekends we were allowed to make our own individual pots. If we were lucky they would be fired. When Janet or Bernard thought we had reached a suitable standard, we were allowed to put them before Bernard, who would then price them or throw them out. It was always an exciting but nervous experience to go in after Bernard had priced them, as in a way it was the ultimate critique on the work. Although Bernard had an excellent eye for good and bad pots, he had a lousy memory for their worth. One week he would price them sky high and another time they would be worth only pennies, it was the same with his own pots. Janet would come along later and readjust the prices closer to the current market values, but the differentials between pots would remain as Bernard had valued them, as this was indicative of their quality.

Bernard had a high regard for his relationship with his students but due to his lack of contact with the workshop, especially in his latter years, he felt there was an increasing distance in his understanding of the people that were coming to study. His early students had been academics and come from the professional classes. They shared much in common experience and background with Bernard, but Janet had long been doing the recruiting and they were now coming from a much broader spectrum of society. People like Trevor and myself were from working class backgrounds able to work there because we were paid a wage. In the past students came to study but did not earn any money at the pottery and some I believe paid for the privilege. In my time the wage structure left little for luxuries, but was just adequate to live on. When you were able to sell pots in the showroom there was even enough to save for emergencies.

Week Ending July 17 1976 — Income Tax Week No. 15

EMPLOYER'S TOTAL GRAD. CONT. FOR THIS WEEK £ ...... N.B. Always Equal To Employees' Total Graduated Contributions For This Week.

NAME	HOURS WORKED 1st Day	2nd Day	3rd Day	4th Day	5th Day	6th Day	7th Day	Total	Rate	Overtime Hours	Overtime Rate	Total Wages Earned	Advances During Week	Deductions or Fines	Nat. Ins. Grad. Cont. Employee
B Yates												15 00			
Marshall								22½		1.	10	24 75			
Gorses								40		1	00	40 00			
Gardner												27 50			
Redding								40		1	00	40 00			
Perry												14 00			
v.d. Berg												16 50			
Stratton												18 00			
Gough												32 50			
												228 25			

NAME	Nat. Ins. Stamp Cont. Employee	Code No.	Total Gross Pay to Date	Total Free Pay to Date Table 'A'	Total Taxable Pay to Date	Total Tax Due to Date Table 'B'	Tax Deducted this Week	Tax Refunded this Week	Total Deductions	Balance due to Employee	National Insurance Total Grad. Cont. to Date Employee	Stamp Contribution Employer
B Yates		684	225 00	198 75	26 25	9 15	60	–	60	14 40		1 3
Marshall		934	277 30	271 50	105.80	36 90	2 25		3 59	21.16	1 34	3
Gorses		674	568 00	196 50	371 50	130 00	9.45		11.76	28 24	2 31	5
Gardner		116	402 50	337 50	65 00	22 75	1 75		3 35	24.15	1.60	4
Redding		674	560 00	196.50	363 50	127 20	9 45		11 76	28 24	2 31	5
Perry		674	210 00	196 50	13 50	4 70	35		1 17	12 83	+82	2 0
v.d. Berg		674	237 50	196 50	41 00	14 35	1 25		2 21	14.29	96	2 4
Stratton		674	270 00	196 50	73 50	25 70	1 75		2 80	15 20	1 05	2 6
Gough		674	477 50	196 50	281 00	98 35	6 85		8 73	23 77	1 88	4 7
							33 70		45 97	182 28	12 27	32

To compensate for his lack of daily contact Bernard invited his students individually for supper. His housekeeper would cook the meal and you would stay all the evening until Bernard got tired, sometimes this could be as late as 11pm. As I was at the pottery for a good few years the conversation could get a little repetitive as Bernard felt he must talk pots to you. As I got used to the pattern I would throw in questions about early life in Japan and China and Bernard would go off into the past, describing in great detail and eloquence his experiences of another world and time. I thought of him as my time machine and was totally captivated by his stories. He also liked and was popular with the ladies and in a spirit of

Wage book 1970s. At this time Bill Marshall was only working a couple of days a week

A small drawing Bernard gave me after my two years apprentice-ship

lads together he let me in on some of his private stories including some revealing ones about Janet. It was at these times he seemed most human and I felt closest to him; he was not performing he was connecting. After a while he would mentally shake himself out of his reverie and continue his lecture, until the next time I could coax him into the past.

His conversation was not all pottery and the crafts; he was also a very religious man. He was of the Baha'i faith an offshoot of Buddhism; he held a high office in the religion and was regularly visited by disciples of the faith. His wanderings into the subject of religion often had him talking about death. It was fascinating to someone on the opposite end of life to hear a person calmly talking about their approaching death. Bernard was not afraid to die he was only afraid he might die before he finished his book 'Beyond East and West.' I clearly remember my last dinner with him before I left for Japan to study for a year. He had filled me with advice and warnings about the delights and difficulties of life in Japan. As I got up to leave I said I would see him again in just over a year's time, he said; "no Johnnie I have just finished my book and it will be time for me to go soon, I will not see you again". He died about six months later while I was in Japan. I have often felt that I would like to have been older and more his equal in our discussions. I would love to have debated with him on his beliefs and philosophy. I always felt they were overly romantic and Arcadian for the time, but then I suppose Bernard came from another time.

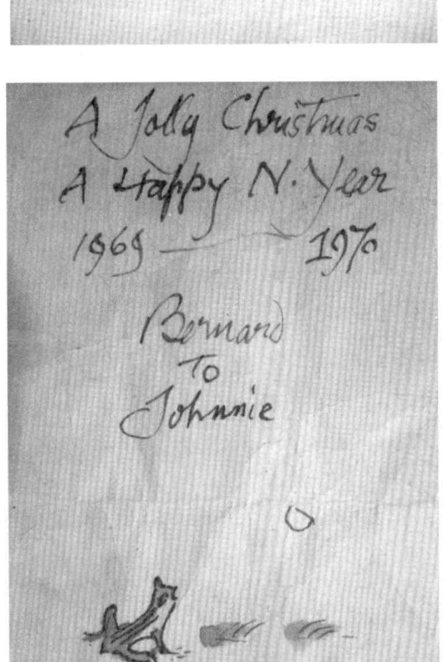

Christmas card sent to me by Bernard

Daily life and duties

Most of the students lived in accommodation supplied by Janet in the centre of St Ives. There were a mixture of rooms and small flats for which we paid a slightly discounted rent. At 8am the pottery van did the rounds picking everyone up to take us about a mile up the Stennack Hill to the pottery. Anchor House where I lived was the first pickup; I would fall in the back and take the opportunity for a few more much needed zzz's before being deposited at the pottery.

Examples of the standard-ware that we made. Medieval jugs, dinner and side plates, general purpose bowls and egg cups

I am sure in earlier years the daily routine in the workshop was a little more earnest, but in my time there was a very relaxed atmosphere and attitude in the throwing room. Bill Marshall regaled us with stories that he made "a hundred egg bakers before morning crib" my target was more like thirty. We were all given 'shapes' to throw, which meant you were responsible for a particular item of the standard-ware. The secretary would post up how many were needed for stock and you were responsible for producing that item all the way through to the first (biscuit) firing, which meant as well as throwing there was; turning, handling, making jug lips, lids and teapot spouts. Students would be allocated their shapes according to their experience. New arrivals would usually start with egg bakers, eggcups, and small dishes, then progress to lidded soup bowls, small gp (general purpose) bowls and small casseroles. The next progression was the larger casseroles, medium and large bowls and jugs.

Bill Marshall threw the largest pots such as extra large bowls and medieval jugs. Bill would supervise you, show you the shape, come along later, tell you to throw them all away and show you again...and again. It was an excellent education as repeat throwing teaches you so much. You have to concentrate all the time on achieving the shape until it becomes automatic; this allows another part of your brain to be able to concentrate on other aspects of the pot. Following the pot through to its finished state is also an important part of your training, as it teaches all the skills needed to make the complete pot.

The biggest influence on me at this time was Bill Marshall. His eye for the shape and his throwing technique were a constant unattainable goal for me. I would secretly watch him throwing to see how he made it work. When he threw you an example of a shape there was always something extra there that you could never achieve, even on the simplest shapes. His individual pots were also an inspiration, when you are learning you will always imitate as a part of the process, it was Bill's pots I found I was unconsciously imitating. Bill rarely gave compliments, neither did I look for them, but if he just grunted and said "not bad boy", you knew you were getting there. For all my admiration for Bill we never really hit it off, over the years we just seemed to tolerate each other which looking back I find rather sad.

Apart from throwing we were given other tasks; there was mixing and pugging the clay, glazing, and packing and firing the kiln. Bernard also would pick someone to paint the 'z' pattern on the large and small porringer. After I had been there a while Bernard picked me for the task. I sat for a week with a Japanese brush and piles of newspaper practicing what looked like a simple three stroke pattern, before I was allowed near the bowls. Although I rarely use a brush in my current work I can still pick up a Japanese brush with a certain amount of confidence, evidence of the value of such training.

Trevor Corser

My other task along with Trevor was to pack and fire the glaze kilns. This was a position of great responsibility as a lot can go wrong in the firing of an oil kiln and the value of the fired kilns depended much on the quality of the firing, especially when there were BL's in it. I so much enjoyed this task, as it was a battle with the elements. No two kilns fired the same, as variables such as the density of the packing and the weather pressure affect the firing. There may also be a larger quantity of ware glazed in tenmoku or celadon and each would need a different style of firing.

Jeff Oestreich. Now a major influence in American ceramics

In the years that Trevor and I were making our individual pots we had running battles with Bill as to positioning them in the kiln. Bill, like us, knew all the best spots and would claim them. He would have priority as his pots were worth more than ours, but if we managed to put our pots in first and quickly pack around them before Bill came out with his, we could sometimes get away with stealing some spots. Often though Bill would say we were packing too fast and make us unpack and repack replacing ours with his.

Firing was a health and safety nightmare by today's standards. The fuel lines were always leaking and we had to put bowls under them to catch the spillage. When the kiln got hot they would ignite and we would have little fires breaking out throughout the firing. Another time we were firing the climbing kiln and we had the wood drying over the fire-mouth. I was in the workshop having lunch with Trevor; he said he would just check the kiln. As he opened the door to the kiln-shed I saw a yellow flickering glow light up his face. The wood had caught fire and there was a merry blaze. Trevor with a pyromaniac's glee rushed to find an extinguisher, he had always wanted

Shigeyoshi Ichino in Tamba, Japan

to try one out, and proceeded to enjoy himself immensely in his role as a fire fighter. We were however always aware of the dangers, and because of the heightened level of awareness I still think these kilns are safer than electric, where people rely on computer controlled cut outs as safety measures.

4pm on Fridays the whole pottery stopped to do the weekly clean up. Floors and surfaces and ware-boards would be washed, your own personal space tidied up, and the kiln-shed and clay-room given the once over. It signalled the end of the week and although you may be coming in over the weekend to do some work on individual pots, there was a party atmosphere about everyone. Most of the students socialised with each other at some time over the weekend. St Ives was a lively place in the 60's and 70's, with many after the pub parties. I remember seeing the Leach crowd out and around before I joined, they looked a compact and somehow elite society and I was envious of their nonchalant camaraderie. Now on the inside there was less of the awe, but even through the years with the constant changes in personnel there was always a strong bond between us all.

John Bedding - my first workshop in Penzance

I left the pottery in 1978 to work and study at the Ichino pottery with my one time friend and colleague Shigeyoshi. The Leach's had arranged it with the Ichinos and I became only the second potter they had sent to Japan. After the easygoing life at the Leach I found my life there complicated and arduous, but in the end rewarding. My friendship with Shigey was stretched to the limit, and although it was arranged that I return to the Leach, I never did. My tough life in Japan taught me how to work seven days a week and long hours, a lesson I needed to learn for starting a workshop of my own.

I always look upon my time at the Leach as being both privileged and one of the most enjoyable times of my life. I, like many, feel I owe a debt to the place and as such I am now working with others to try to bring it into public ownership and preserve its unique spirit for the benefit of future generations.

The Leach Pottery

Marion Whybrow

'We want from the artist potter the same sort of quality which we expect from a good author, poet, painter or composer. Your main objective should be aesthetic, to know good pot from bad pot and to be able to find your way with your own clear convictions amidst all the good and bad pots past and present to making good sincere and honest pots of your own.'

This is part of a letter from Bernard Leach addressed to his grandson, John, in 1960 in preparing him to meet the commitment and strict requirements that Leach demanded of anyone who came to work at St Ives Pottery, whether clay mixer, apprentice, student, or experienced potter.

After Bernard Leach and Shoji Hamada set up the pottery in 1920 in St Ives, Cornwall, students began clamouring to work there. Applicants were interviewed and a short trial period arranged when they were carefully judged for their suitability and persistence in learning to develop skills through the necessary work routine of making standard-ware. The experience of learning to throw a pot to a determined shape, size and weight, was essential before the development of individual expression. This Leach encouraged through his careful analysis of their pots and in the student acquiring techniques and a critical eye for the aesthetics of form, shape and balance.

Leach felt there was an essential quality that came from throwing and repeating a shape and learning to handle clay. The pots he admired were Korean and Chinese, made by simple craftsmen. He firmly believed that a rhythm developed within the potter through the repeat process which gave life to a pot. 'I used to be able to tell which person made the pots in my pottery - the standardware of cups and bowls and plates. There were eight or ten people working and sometimes I would go around and see some of their work on a shelf and I would say to myself the character of the person who made that is coming through. That is what I want to see. It is a very important thing.' [1] The central core in Bernard's belief was 'the pot is the man.'

In his final book *Beyond East and West* Leach wrote, 'Gradually from all over the world we must have had nearly a hundred students, but there was never any attempt to start anything like classes, as done in schools and American Universities. Periodically I talked to them as they learnt their alphabets of clay - its qualities - its innate demands on a potter - its form and decoration - kiln, slips, glazes, encouraging them to stand on their own feet, both technically and aesthetically, insisting on right standards, but avoiding rules.' [2]

Warren MacKenzie and his wife Alix were the first Americans to become pupils at the Leach Pottery after the second World War. Warren, on teaching pottery in Art School in America said, 'When I taught second year students, who thought they were pretty good and could throw, to show them their weaknesses I produced one of the Leach standard shapes. Make one correctly this term was the assignment. No one ever could.' [3] This underlined Bernard's firm conviction that the workshop was the proper place for learning craft skills.

Bernard Leach loading Japanese climbing kiln at St Ives 1920s

The beginning

The St Ives Pottery reaches back to 1920, when Leach, having spent eleven years in China and Japan, was leaving the East to set up a pottery in England with his friend Shoji Hamada, the Japanese potter. It says much for the friendship of the two men that they travelled across the world together to an uncertain future. Certainly for a Japanese man to leave his country was unusual in 1920, and so began a fusion of the art and traditions of East and West, a successful marriage of two different cultures.

At that time The St Ives Handicraft Guild, wished to include a potter and its founder Mrs Frances Horne, put up £2,500 which Leach matched with a similar sum over a period of time, enabling him to buy a property. The chosen site for the building was three quarters of a mile up hill from St Ives in Cornwall, where a large artists' colony had flourished since the 1880s and was (and still is) one of the foremost colonies in Britain. At the turn of the 20th century 30 artists from St Ives had their work hung in the Royal Academy.

The arrival of the artists, who rented net lofts for studios, preserved the old cottages in the fishing quarter and

The three chambered climbing kiln

Chamber of the kiln packed for firing

employed much of the population, helped ensure the town's economic survival. The Stennack stream, by which the pottery was built, carried the sediment of old tin mines down to the sea and small town harbour, once famous for its fishing industry.

Leach and Hamada identified with the Arts and Crafts movement of William Morris and the making of functional ware for the ordinary household, but in practice they began producing individual studio pots, designed largely for exhibition in galleries, rather than creating a country workshop of domestic ware to sell from the premises. They built a Japanese, wood fired, three chambered climbing kiln on a slope, the first of its kind in Britain, enabling the potter to fire one chamber after another with varying temperatures. Each chamber measured 180 centimetres height and width, by 120 centimetres front to back. Cornwall had long been denuded of its trees and finding fuel for the kiln was one of their first difficulties, as well as the search for local clays and natural materials for glazes. Together they tramped the countryside in their quest for these vital elements.

Leach kick wheel

Bill Marshall at the wheel

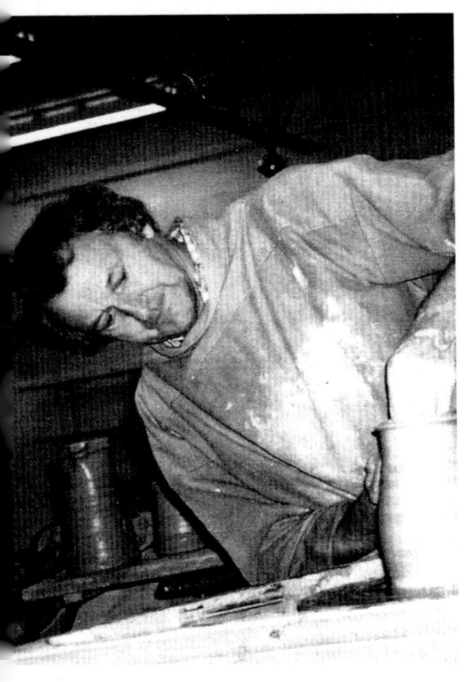

The building of the pottery aroused the curiosity of local people. It had been reported that an industrial plant was being established which would solve the unemployment problems of the town. Leach wrote to the St Ives Times explaining the position.

'Sir: As there seem to be various rumours in the town that the pottery which we are now building below Penbeagle Farm is to be a large industrial concern, employing local labour, I shall be glad of the opportunity of briefly stating the facts in order to prevent any sense of disappointment which might otherwise arise.'

'The works are to be of a private nature and on quite a small scale. For the first year or two, at least, we shall not employ more than the occasional odd labour of one or two men. How the work will develop later on remains to be seen. Our object is to turn out genuine, handicrafts of quality rather than machine craft in quantity.'

'The former is difficult to find now in England, as it has been driven out by modern industry and applied science. In the Cornish pitcher, made at the Lake Pottery at Truro, it is still possible to see something of the spirit of the old English pottery, but the ware is a very simple one and unsuited to many modern purposes. I have long been studying pottery in the Far East, where the traditions of old craftsmanship and beauty have not yet been driven out, and the various kinds of earthenware, stoneware and porcelain, which my Japanese friend and assistant, Mr Hamada and I will make, will be an attempt to combine the fine old craft of both East and West to our present needs. With many thanks for the courtesy of your page.

Yours truly, Bernard Leach.' [4]

After the completion of the building, which Leach and Hamada had designed themselves, one of the workmen, George Dunn, ex miner and fisherman, offered his services as general labourer for the pottery. This help was welcomed by Leach and Hamada, who were building the interior, constructing the kiln, digging for clay and searching for wood. George soon found himself sawing 200 tons of wood for the kiln, bought from the Great Western Railway, and helping to make benches, shelving, and other necessary equipment. He remained a loyal worker for nearly 28 years. His son Horatio took over in 1937 until his retirement in 1958. Horatio died in 1994. One of the early potters, Valerie Bond, wrote to tell me (the author) of the importance of George and Horatio Dunn to the pottery. 'If it had not been for their hard work with the clay, there would have been no pots. Horatio's sense of humour kept us all going on difficult days, and we all owed a great deal to him. He also packed the pots for sending away – a very responsible job.'

Bernard bought the 14-roomed Count House in Carbis Bay for his wife, Muriel, three girls and two boys. David and Michael, both became potters. Grandson John, also became a potter and subsequently, his sons. The house was once owned by the captain of Wheal Providence tin mine. It had also been the home of psychologist, Dr Havelock Ellis, president of the World League for Sexual Reform, and his wife Edith, who raised prize bulls on the small portion of land round the house, and wrote novels in the vernacular about the local population of St Ives.

Top: *Horatio Dunn kneading clay*

Above: *The Count House, Carbis Bay, Leach family home*

Left: *The Pottery Cottage, St Ives*

The working partnership

Leach and Hamada at Mashiko

Shoji made his home at the pottery. Leach and Hamada enjoyed working together, talking over meals round the open fireplace, sharing the same ideals and values, learning from each other and their experience of making pots and so fusing their ideas of the meeting of two cultures. They were producing English slipware and Oriental stoneware and hard porcelain. Leach considered that he, Hamada and Cardew revived the technique of seventeenth century English slipware, which was rediscovered accidentally when Leach and Hamada sliced through a sandwich of blackberry jam and cream and saw how the substances fused.

But the beginning was essentially an experimental period when they made mistakes, with many of their firings ending up smashed in the Stennack stream. But they were pioneers and felt they were establishing the era of the artist-craftsman potter, the educated artist taking up a job which was previously relegated to the village workshop. The thinking man would replace the artisan's hand-made craft which had been swept away by the Industrial Revolution, when all pots were made to perfection and in thousands, and reinstate the idea of truth to materials and an appreciation of the beauty of simple design, quiet colours and the personal touch. They both admired Korean and Chinese ceramics, as well as mediaeval English pots and early Japanese tea ware.

1946 Leach Pottery discussion, Mary Gibson Horrocks, Bernard, Valerie Bond, David Leach

The high cost of kiln losses meant the pots were fairly expensive but both Leach and Hamada managed to exhibit locally, on Show Day, when artists opened their studios to the general public, and in the Cotswold and Paterson Galleries in Bond Street, London. They also sold their pots to Japan. Their Japanese friends were sending generous amounts of money to Cornwall from sales to help finance the pottery. However, in Britain sales were poor. The pots were considered faulty because of the impurities in the natural clays, textures, and the variations in the glazes, compared with the smooth perfection achieved by industrial methods of production. An American collector, Henry Bergen, acquired many of their early experimental pots. As well as introducing them to other collectors, he came to St Ives and joined enthusiastically in kiln firings, as did other friends who were prepared to help round the clock at a time when firings could take up to 36 hours.

Right: *1947 Pottery crew. Kenneth Quick, David Leach, Joe Benney, Bernard, Mary Gibson Horrocks, Eileen Newton, Horatio Nelson Dunn*

Left: *1948 Pottery crew Joe Benney, Michael Leach, Frank Vibert, Margaret Leach, Joyce Laity, Horatio Dunn, Bill Marshall, Kenneth Quick, Cecil Baugh, Anne-Marie Backer Mohr*

Raku

Leach began his study of raku in Tokyo and, after being established a few years, used the technique to help advertise the pottery in St Ives. The public were invited to attend afternoon demonstrations of low temperature Japanese raku-fired pots in a small purpose-built kiln. They decorated their

Bernard judging pots on the shelf

biscuit purchases and watched as they were glazed and fired and afterwards carried them home. It didn't actually achieve much in extra sales. Bernard had intended to extend hospitality: 'teas of a good home-made character will be provided in the pottery cottage now being built. The furnishing of the new room will be by some of the best English craftsmen and women.' [5] The teas were provided and good Cornish fare served by Muriel, Bernard's first wife, but the proposed furnishing of the room did not materialise.

Leach did in fact design furniture. The first instance had been a chair made in Japan to support his long legs. Over six feet in height, he had grown tired of sitting on the floor, Japanese style. For the pottery he designed a modified version of the kick wheel which was made in wood by Robin Nance, a local furniture maker, and which is still in use at the pottery. It seems to have been manufactured commercially at some time and advertised as the 'modified Leach Pottery wheel.'

Stoneware plate, willow tree pattern 18cm diameter. Preserve pot decorated with leaf motif 12.5cm. Both decorated by Bernard Leach

After little more than three years the Japanese climbing kiln was in a state of collapse because of their inexperience and the varieties of wood used which created choking in the firing and problems with the glazes. Fortunately, Tsuronosuke Matsubayashi, an engineer and kiln specialist, and the product of 39 generations of family potters in Kyoto, arrived from Japan. He rebuilt and redesigned the three-chambered climbing kiln to a more efficient standard. During his stay in St Ives he exhibited with the local Print Society 'a study of Japanese medlars.' He remained at the pottery until l924. Hamada returned to Japan in 1923, after an earthquake had devastated the city of Tokyo and he was unable to contact his family. Hamada married in Japan and built his own kiln in Mashiko in 1930, where four boys and two girls were born. Two of the boys, Shinsaku and Atsuya, became potters and a grandson, Tomoo, son of Shinsaku. They all came to St Ives.

In Mashiko Hamada adopted the lifestyle of a Zen monk and the belief that where he lived and worked was the place he achieved a higher dimension. His pots were linked to daily life and usefulness.

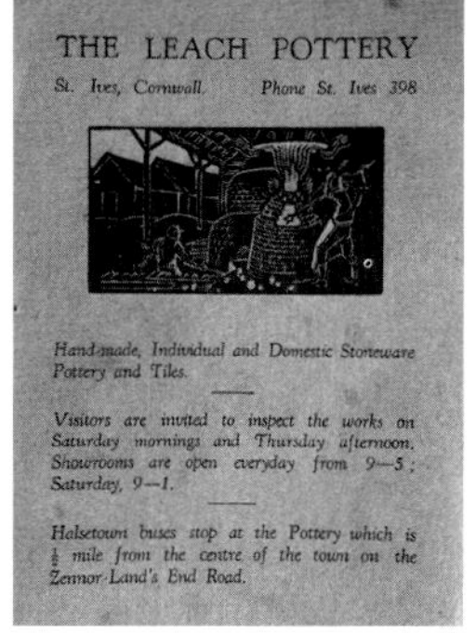

THE LEACH POTTERY

St. Ives, Cornwall. Phone St. Ives 398

Hand-made, Individual and Domestic Stoneware Pottery and Tiles.

Visitors are invited to inspect the works on Saturday mornings and Thursday afternoon. Showrooms are open everyday from 9—5; Saturday, 9—1.

Halsetown buses stop at the Pottery which is ½ mile from the centre of the town on the Zennor-Land's End Road.

***Top:** Part coffee set made by Bernard Leach*

***Above left:** Leach Pottery preserve pot on cover of catalogue*

***Above right:** Cover of catalogue*

Hamada liked to call himself, simply, 'a potter.' One tradition that Hamada took back to Mashiko was the Cornish Pasty, a shell-shaped pastry case filled with chopped beef and vegetables. According to Tomoo, his grandson, it is still made and appreciated in Mashiko.

Bernard Leach firing the kiln at St Ives

The first students and others

Leach crew grinding pots

In 1923 the pottery almost accidentally acquired its first student when Michael Cardew, who decided he wanted to work with Leach, turned up on his doorstep at the Count House with Shoji Hamada, who had accompanied him there from the pottery. Cardew was not totally without experience of potting but on meeting Bernard soon realised, 'what I naturally liked was not necessarily the last word, and that many kinds of pot which were at first inaccessible to me had qualities which I would be able to learn about if I tried.' [6]

Cardew felt he wasn't entirely acceptable to Leach on their first acquaintance. Fortunately they shared an enthusiasm for English slipware and so in July 1923, after finishing his studies at Oxford, he joined the staff. He was at first disheartened by his inability to throw an order for two dozen mugs to a uniform size and shape and learnt that, 'unless you can do this you are only an improviser, not a thrower.'[7]

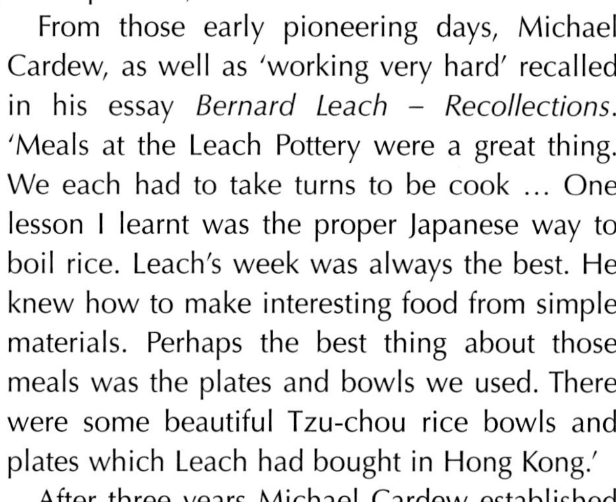

From those early pioneering days, Michael Cardew, as well as 'working very hard' recalled in his essay *Bernard Leach – Recollections*. 'Meals at the Leach Pottery were a great thing. We each had to take turns to be cook … One lesson I learnt was the proper Japanese way to boil rice. Leach's week was always the best. He knew how to make interesting food from simple materials. Perhaps the best thing about those meals was the plates and bowls we used. There were some beautiful Tzu-chou rice bowls and plates which Leach had bought in Hong Kong.'

After three years Michael Cardew established his own pottery at Winchcombe in Gloucestershire. In 1939, from a dilapidated property, he built the Wenford Bridge Pottery at

Michael Cardew at the Leach pottery 1925

Bodmin in Cornwall, which for many years was worked by his son Seth and grandson Ara.

Students continued to arrive. They came for a matter of weeks or a year or two. Several skilled potters arrived with the primary aim of having access to Bernard and for the experience of working at the Leach Pottery. Others studied at art school and worked there part time. Henry Hammond spent two weeks with Bernard just after the Second World War before teaching at West Surrey College of Art. He had studied pottery under William Staite Murray at the Royal College of Art, London, after attending design courses run by Edward Bawden and Eric Ravilious. Helen Pincombe worked for six weeks at the St Ives pottery before becoming a student of William Staite Murray. She taught at Guildford and Willesden Schools of Art. She ran her own workshop in Oxshott, Surrey from 1949 until she retired in 1972. Staite Murray visited St Ives in 1923, when Hamada taught him to make footrings to his pots. Both Pincombe and Murray taught at the Royal College of Art.

Dinah Dunn (Batterham) potting at St Ives 1954

Katharine Pleydell-Bouverie spent an anxious fortnight, on trial, before being taken on. Norah Braden joined later and according to Bernard was one of the most sensitive of students to work at the pottery. Others for short periods were Charlotte Epton, she married the war artist Edward Bawden. Barbara Millard, died in South Africa. William Worrall and John Coney potted at Glastonbury and Kenneth Murray trained potters in Nigeria.

Another visitor was Lucie Rie, who visited Bernard at Dartington, and also travelled down from London to St Ives, making her buttons and beads at the bench. Mary Gibson-Horrocks remembers, 'I sat next to her handling my jugs and was fascinated with her work.' Lucie Rie's buttons are exhibited in the fashion collection of the Victoria and Albert Museum, London. The delicacy and elegance of her pots is in

Sylvia Hardaker sealing kiln for individual firing

sharp contrast to those of Leach, but they admired each other's work. Bernard would often stay with Lucie, in her Albion Mews studio flat on his trips to London, and she stayed at Bernard's flat in Barnaloft when in St Ives. Artist Willie Barns Graham remembers her sitting outside her window on Porthmeor beach.

Michael Leach, although familiar with the pottery from an early age, joined Bernard and David in 1950, but set up his own pottery five years later. David Leach joined his father at the pottery in 1930 and was taught to throw by Muriel Bell, later to establish a pottery at Malvern. He was also instructed by Harry Davis from whom David said he learned more throwing skills than anyone else. Paul Barron, who later taught at Farnham College of Art with Henry Hammond, was taught by two Leach potters, Norah Braden and Helen Pincombe. John Bew arrived at the pottery in 1938 and later joined a Quaker school and taught pottery skills to boys from a local mining community in the Rhondda. In 1942 he supplied pottery for John Lewis store in London from the Odney Pottery at Cookham-on-Thames, Berkshire. Anthony Richards, running his own pottery in St Ives, called on Bernard to discuss pots and for conversations on art versus crafts.

Kenneth Quick at Tregenna Hill Pottery

Nirmala Patwardhan, born in Hyderabad, India, in 1928, worked with Bernard in the late fifties and also with Ray Finch at the Winchcombe Pottery, where she conducted a number of her glaze experiments. In 1984 she published *Handbook for Potters* intended for potters working in India. Her enlarged *New Handbook for Potters* was published in 2005.

Brenda Potter, nee Tinklin, worked for 18 months at the Leach Pottery from 1978-1980. 'When I started John Bedding, Trevor Corser and Jason Wason were there. Most of the memories are of chatting round the fire. The big event was the death of Bernard and sitting round Janet's table with Trevor and Jason and talking for hours.' Before joining Leach Brenda had served a two-year apprenticeship at the Mask Pottery in Penzance and before

David Leach lifting a thrown pot from the wheel head

doing a BA Hons in Fine Art at Ravensbourne College in Kent. She went on to teach ceramics and art and became head of a comprehensive school in Portsmouth; 'but my first love is still ceramics. I have a wheel and kiln at home and still do commissions.'

Alix Mackenzie decorating pot late 1950s

Left: *Peter Hardy pouring glaze*

Below: *Peter Woods handling soup bowls*

Left: *Bernard Leach decorating pots*

Pots on show in the pottery porch

Artists and societies

Soon after arriving in St Ives Bernard Leach and family, and Hamada, joined the St Ives Arts Club, a professional club for painters, musicians, architects, writers and sculptors. During those early years Bernard and various members of the family took as their guests, Matsubayashi, Michael Cardew, Norah Braden, Katharine Pleydell-Bouverie, Ada Mason, William Worrall, Muriel Bell, John Coney, Bernard Forrester, Valerie Bond, Dick Kendall, Patrick Heron, Mary Gibson-Horrocks and Beryl Debney, all of whom worked at the pottery at various times. The Leach family enjoyed a long association with the Arts Club and friends of the children were allowed access to clay and the wheel at the pottery.

In 1926 St Ives Society of Artists was established from a break-away group of the Arts Club where, Bernard said at a meeting, they should have a gallery to display their work. The first exhibition space was set up in the Porthmeor studios. In 1949, following an acrimonious split between the modern and traditionalist factions in the Society, the Penwith Society of Arts was formed by the modern artists with Ben Nicholson and Barbara Hepworth at their head. Bernard and David Leach were among them, both exhibiting frequently in the Society and serving on the committee in the early sixties.

Bernard was active in the artists' community in working for the good of the town and its environment. In the early 1960s he was among many famous artist signatories in a letter to *The Times* protesting at the Admiralty's plans to use the moorland, an area of outstanding natural beauty, for troop landing exercises. Leach, Hepworth and Heron also joined forces with Friends of the Earth to block planning permission, for a holiday complex at a former clay works, in which they were successful. In 1962 Bernard Leach was awarded the CBE in the New Year's Honours list to mark his 50 years as a potter. He was on a lecture tour in New Zealand when the news came through. CBEs were also awarded to Barbara Hepworth in 1958 and to Patrick Heron 1977. In 1968 Leach, Hepworth and Nicholson were granted the Freedom of the Borough of St Ives in recognition of their services to the town and their international contribution to the arts. Exhibitions of pottery, sculpture and painting were held throughout St Ives in celebration.

Lidded stew pot with ears, stoneware, and dishes

Right: *Leach Pottery catalogue 1954, page two*

Above: *Leach Pottery catalogue 1954, page one*

Cecil Baugh with Horatio Dunn 1949

Dartington

In 1927 Bernard and Muriel Leach drove to Devon to see Dorothy and Leonard Elmhirst, who were establishing a progressive school and a centre for rural arts and crafts in a beautiful but run down mediaeval estate at Dartington Hall. Dorothy invited Bernard Leach to transfer his pottery there and join the community but, instead, he recommended Sylvia Fox-Strangways, who had worked at St Ives, to run their first pottery classes. Sylvia retired in 1929, because of ill health, but remained in close association with Dartington throughout her life. Examples of her work can be seen at Dartington Hall, where some of the fire surrounds are decorated with her tiles.

In 1931/32 Leach did establish a small workshop there producing traditional slipware and taught part-time at the Foxhole School at Dartington, while the Elmhirsts built a new pottery at Shinners Bridge, close by the estate. Before its completion Bernard was in Japan and David Leach was the first teacher at the pottery. A year later, in 1934, the Elmhirsts sponsored David for a management and scientific course at Stoke Technical College in the heart of industrial pottery. He undertook this with the intention of improving output and efficiency at the Dartington Pottery. Bernard Forrester, who had been working at St Ives, moved to Dartington to teach, while the Leach Pottery was run by Harry Davis, who carried the main burden of production in the years 1933-37. Bernard Leach described Harry as 'the only fast, well-trained thrower on the potter's wheel who had ever studied with me.'[8] May Scott joined the small team and eventually married Harry.

From Stoke-on-Trent David did not return to Dartington, but to St Ives. Having acquired knowledge and confidence, he developed some of the techniques learned in industry and applied them to the small pottery. With financial help from Dartington a certain amount of modernisation took place, including a change to oil firing and the introduction of machinery to reduce time in preparing clay. He also gave up slipware in favour of the more adaptable stoneware. Another lesson learned was

David Leach with Horatio Dunn, St Ives 1950

that if the pottery was to run smoothly a more permanent staff would be needed. They decided to recruit and train local boys straight from school. The first apprentice was William Marshall, who joined the staff in 1938 and became a skilled thrower, teacher, foreman, and mainstay of the Leach Pottery for about 40 years.

Bill Marshall with Helena da Silva (Klug) c1957

Bernard Leach in Japan

In Japan a craft movement, named Mingei (art of the people), was forming and Leach was invited to visit by the leader, his close friend Soetsu Yanagi. In 1934 Dorothy Elmhirst generously financed the trip and provided the money for Mark Tobey, an American painter, to go as travelling companion. He and Bernard had become friends when they were teaching at Dartington. It was Tobey who introduced Leach to the Baha'i faith, which, attracted by their belief in the brotherhood of man, Bernard then followed to the end of his days.

While in Japan Leach took the opportunity of visiting potteries in remote areas, learning to improvise with the materials to hand. At Mashiko he was hosted by Hamada's family. The friends renewed their pleasure in potting together and firing the kilns. Years later, in 1957, Hamada's son Atsuya came to work in St Ives and his second son, Shinsaku, visited with Hamada in 1963. Hamada returned to Britain several times and in 1966 he brought his wife Kazue and daughter. The cosmopolitan team working at the Leach Pottery at that time - from Canada, Australia, Scandinavia and America - were honoured to meet him.

Bernard with Mirek Smisek 1963

At Kyoto Leach explored the workshops of Kanjiro Kawai, who had an eight chambered kiln. Here Leach made porcelain pots. In Tokyo he resumed a working relationship with Kenkichi Tomimoto with whom he shared the title of 7th Kenzan inherited from their Japanese Pottery Master

Ogata Kenzan in 1912. At Matsue, on Lake Shinji, he met the potter Michitada Funaki, whose son Kenji came to England for a year in 1967 to work with David Leach at Lowerdown Pottery in Devon and again in 1977 to visit Bernard at St Ives.

At Abiko Leach renewed his friendship with the Yanagi family on whose land he had built a kiln and workroom in 1917. He learnt of the construction of a folk craft museum being planned by Yanagi, Kawai and Hamada in Tokyo. Their idea was to find and exhibit domestic handmade crafts in cloth, metalwork, lacquer, furniture, prints, pots, and every available artefact made by the 'unknown craftsman.' Their intention was to raise the level of these traditional crafts, which were under threat from Japan's desperate bid to launch itself into the modern world. Leach played a major role and travelled hundreds of miles with Yanagi, Hamada and Kawai choosing and collecting samples of country crafts for exhibition in Tokyo and Osaka. In 1929 Yanagi had founded the Japanese Craft Movement, the same year as he and Hamada visited England. In 1936 Yanagi's dream of establishing a Japanese Folkcraft Museum in Tokyo was realised.

Nirmala Patwardhan and Bernard at a kiln opening 1962

A Potters Book

Leach's experiences in Japan led him to write *A Potter's Book* and Dorothy Elmhirst, as well as sponsoring his trip to Japan, also provided the means for his research and working time for writing the book. It was published in 1940 and has been invaluable to anyone determined to follow the craft. It has been translated into many languages and never out of print. As well as being a practical text book it has proved an inspiration to aspiring potters. 'I felt there was a gap. I saw the

Bill Marshall putting a lip on a jug

Leach Pottery workshop

need for interpretation, and with the hope of assisting young English potters, began to write *A Potter's Book*. Fortunately I had always kept diaries and notes covering standards, methods and ideals. I had no idea of the wide response the book would receive.' [9]

Too many to name have been converted to ceramics through reading the book, which soon acquired the status of 'The Potter's Bible'. Michael Casson was one who succumbed to its influence. He later taught pottery at Harrow School of Art. Eileen Lewenstein, in her final year of teacher training at London University, read the book, gained experience as a potter, set up a studio in Hampstead and taught pottery at Hornsey College of Art. Ray Finch, who took over the Winchcombe Pottery from Michael Cardew, acknowledged the book's importance in his formative years.

1952 Leach Pottery crew. David Leach, Bernard, Frank Vibert, Michael Leach, Bill Marshall, Joe Benney, Kenneth Quick, Sheila Mitchell, Walter Firth, Horatio Dunn, Alix Mackenzie

Leach designed tiles on the gravestone of Edgar Skinner, business manager of pottery 1922, Barnoon cemetery, St Ives

The Irish potter, Peter Brennan wrote to Bernard through the publisher and on visiting the Leach Pottery was invited by David and Bernard to become an apprentice. He turned down the offer, having established a pottery studio with Victor Waddington. However, on the death of David Leach in 2005, Helena Brennan, widow of Peter wrote, 'The passing of David Leach brings into focus the generous help and encouragement given by the Leach family to the development of the current thriving pottery scene here in Ireland. My late husband, Peter Brennan 1916-1995, called himself "a correspondent student of David's" with whom he had a lifelong friendship. I myself was trained to make spectacular tea pots at Lowerdown.' Molly Attrill, potter from the Isle of Wight, says she was 'steeped in the Leach St Ives ethos,' through reading the book, which prompted her to go on a Leach pilgrimage. Michael Leach taught her to pot. She then studied at West Surrey College of Art and Design, Farnham, under Henry Hammond. There she met Marcia Cox, a former Leach student, and helped her set up her pottery in Ontario, Canada.

Although Leach guided students in aesthetics, standards, the use of basic materials and a genuine love for the craft in his teaching and writing, he did not want to produce copyists. In a letter to Warren MacKenzie in 1968 Bernard wrote, 'I don't expect Lucie Rie or Michael Cardew or Hans Coper or Hamada to like, or do, just what I like or do.' Three of the potters he most admired owed nothing to his style and technique. Janet Leach was an American whose pots he described as strong, free and adventurous. Lucie Rie came from Vienna and her work was quiet and refined, reflecting her personality. Hans Coper from Germany showed positive modern traits with references to older roots. He felt their backgrounds allowed them a certain cultural freedom. However, a tradition did grow from Bernard's teachings and he attracted many admirers and followers. For himself, Leach said he enjoyed pulling a handle on a pot and was probably more proficient in this technique than in throwing.

Horse and Rider by Bernard Leach intended for roof ridge

The war years

Favourite motifs for Bernard's decorated pots

During the war years David and Bill Marshall were serving in the forces while Bernard joined the Home Guard along with the artists Adrian Stokes, Leonard Fuller, Denis Mitchell and Borlase Smart. Leach, by now divorced from Muriel, married his second wife, Laurie Cookes, who was secretary at the pottery. They too eventually separated and divorced. Two conscientious objectors who were detailed to work at the pottery were Dick Kendall - who later taught at Camberwell College of Art and married Bernard's daughter Jessamine - and Patrick Heron, art critic and painter. Heron had lived in St Ives as a child and in the fifties he and his wife Delia bought Eagles Nest, a house on a promontory on the road to Zennor, formerly the home of landscape painter and politician, Will Arnold-Forster and his wife, Ka Cox, friend of Virginia Woolf. Heron was commissioned to design a stained glass window for the opening of the Tate Gallery, St Ives in 1993.

Heron spent 14 months at the pottery and said of Bernard, 'He has demonstrated the aesthetic parallel existing between Sung and mediaeval English pottery - thus creating a genuine East-West synthesis; and, in doing this, he has given us a ceramic idiom very much in accord with aspects of modern art. One can compare him to Henry Moore in some ways: both by-passed the Renaissance.' [10]

In 1941 Edward Bouverie-Hoyton, principal of Penzance School of Arts set up a pottery department and Bernard Leach was the first potter to teach there. Sons David and Michael Leach were also later to teach at Penzance.

The Leach Pottery was out of action for a time during the war when a stray bomb partly demolished the cottage and workshop. Ironically, there was a demand for domestic pots.

Fish tile

Bernard fluting a jug

Four women worked at the pottery in the war years, Aileen Newton, Valerie Bond, Mary Gibson-Horrocks and namesake Margaret Leach. Mary, Valerie and Bernard lived in the pottery cottage and Margaret lived opposite, but all shared the household chores. Bernard, whose task was to do the laundry, drew up a list of duties.

After the war Grattan Freyer and his French wife Madeleine joined them from Ireland. David returned, and with his acquired skills from the Stoke factories, introduced oil firing and technical improvements to increase production. He set up a three year apprenticeship scheme, taking local youths. Bill Marshall, who joined the pottery in 1938 became a team leader. Bernard Made the prototypes and drew them on cards with dimensions for whoever was making cups, saucers, bowls, jugs and other items. Bernard and David designed a range of Leach Standard Ware with a catalogue.

Decorated plate

Preserve jar

In 1942, Alfred Wallis, the primitive St Ives painter died. Bernard Leach joined Adrian Stokes and Margaret Mellis, Ben Nicholson, Miriam and Naum Gabo and the writer George Manning-Sanders among those attending the funeral. Later, Leach made a ceramic tiled panel for his grave in Barnoon cemetery, showing a figure entering a lighthouse. It reads, 'Alfred Wallis Artist and Mariner'. Wallis turned painter at the age of 70 as a refuge from loneliness after the death of his wife. His untutored style was much admired by the modern painters, especially Ben Nicholson and Christopher Wood who had discovered Wallis on an excursion to St Ives in 1928. Jim Ede, then assistant curator at the Tate Gallery, London, bought many of Wallis's paintings which can now be seen, along with Leach pots and work by other St Ives artists, at Kettle's Yard, Cambridge. Jim Ede gifted his house and collection of paintings, pottery and sculpture, to the University of Cambridge.

Leach designed tiles on gravestone of Alfred Wallis, painter, Barnoon cemetery, St Ives

Bernard and David form a partnership

Invitation to a talk by Bernard Leach at the Berkeley Galleries

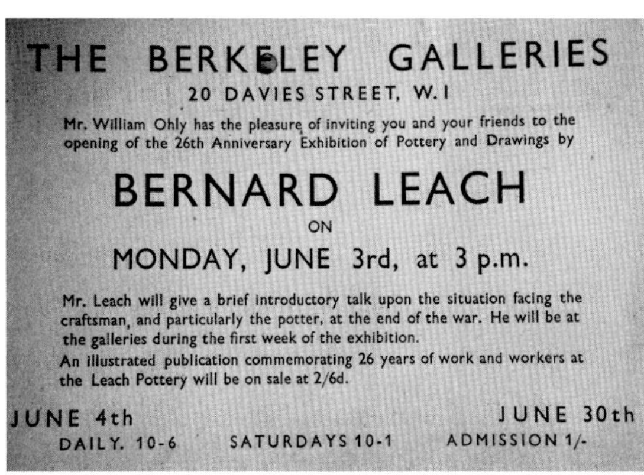

THE BERKELEY GALLERIES

20 DAVIES STREET, W.1

Mr. William Ohly has the pleasure of inviting you and your friends to the opening of the 26th Anniversary Exhibition of Pottery and Drawings by

BERNARD LEACH

ON

MONDAY, JUNE 3rd, at 3 p.m.

Mr. Leach will give a brief introductory talk upon the situation facing the craftsman, and particularly the potter, at the end of the war. He will be at the galleries during the first week of the exhibition.
An illustrated publication commemorating 26 years of work and workers at the Leach Pottery will be on sale at 2/6d.

JUNE 4th JUNE 30th

DAILY. 10-6 SATURDAYS 10-1 ADMISSION 1/-

David returned from war service and went into partnership with Bernard in 1946. They were joined by Michael Leach in 1950 and there followed a period of stability to 1955. Demand for Leach standard-ware in the post war years grew to such an extent that London stores like Heals, Liberty and John Lewis wanted everything they could produce. David was now largely responsible for the organisation and running of the pottery, but the guiding hand was Bernard's, and pots were still made to his design and purpose. David said, "He was always the artist, creator and inspiration. I was the right hand man. Bernard would make the first pot and I would make the first interpretation. I taught the team of people."[11] The partnership continued happily for 25 years. When David and Michael left in 1955 to set up their own separate potteries in Devon, Bill Marshall became foreman in charge of the team.

A catalogue from the time shows over 100 items from egg cups to casseroles, along with individual pots, 'the personal work of Bernard or David Leach or other members of the Pottery, whose seal they usually bear.'[12] Staffing levels were increased and joining as an apprentice in 1945 was Kenneth Quick, a local lad, and Joe Benney, who became the glazer and glaze maker and a vital addition to the working life of the potters, who relied on Joe's expertise and preparation of the glazes.

The first post-war exhibition of individual pots was held at the Berkeley Gallery in London in 1946. The invitation was designed by the printer, Guido Morris, with the words running down the paper to replicate Japanese writing. Morris was working in St Ives at the time and designed many artists' catalogues and exhibition posters, including

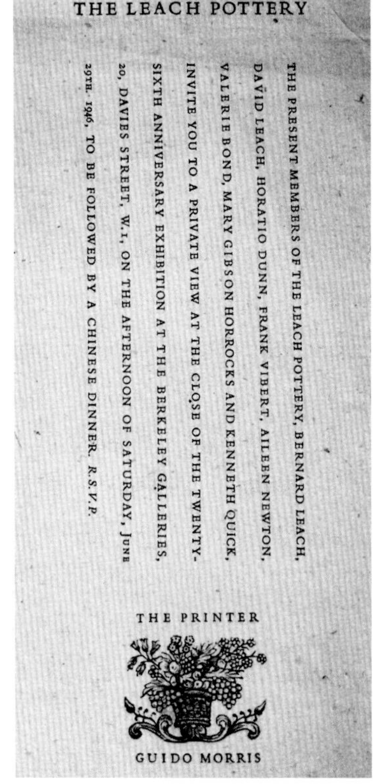

THE LEACH POTTERY

THE PRESENT MEMBERS OF THE LEACH POTTERY, BERNARD LEACH,
DAVID LEACH, HORATIO DUNN, FRANK VIBERT, AILEEN NEWTON,
VALERIE BOND, MARY GIBSON HORROCKS AND KENNETH QUICK,
INVITE YOU TO A PRIVATE VIEW AT THE CLOSE OF THE TWENTY-
SIXTH ANNIVERSARY EXHIBITION AT THE BERKELEY GALLERIES,
20, DAVIES STREET, W.1, ON THE AFTERNOON OF SATURDAY, JUNE
29TH. 1946, TO BE FOLLOWED BY A CHINESE DINNER. *R.S.V.P.*

THE PRINTER

GUIDO MORRIS

Printed invitation to the Berkeley Gallery designed by Guido Morris 1946

the famous 'Catalo' for the Crypt Group set up by Sven Berlin, Peter Lanyon and John Wells. A photograph taken outside the Berkeley gallery shows artists, friends, exhibitors, relatives and students. Afterwards they lunched at a Chinese restaurant in Soho, before going on to the BBC for the showing of a film taken at the St Ives Pottery. Mary Gibson-Horrocks remembers that about 30 people attended and afterwards they all went back to Lucie Rie's flat for tea and her famous sponge cake.

Valerie Bond, working at the pottery during 1946 described Bernard Leach as, 'The father to all the artists. Many of the young and struggling artists, now in the Tate, used to visit the pottery. It was the home they loved to come to. They were all glad to talk to Bernard.' [13] They went there at tea time and in the evenings. The visitors included the painters Ben Nicholson and Adrian Stokes, the printer, Guido Morris, other potters working in the town, and the sculptors, Barbara Hepworth, Sven Berlin and Naum Gabo. 'One memorable day Gabo spoke to some of us for two hours in his studio about his work and the Constructivist movement.' [14] Valerie recalls the first time she met Gabo. 'Bernard said he was taking us to see a friend. We walked across the fields and the door of the bungalow was opened by an excited little man. He just said, "Come and See" and led us through to a room, which was unlit except for the moon shining through a construction he had just made. We all stood there in silence and amazement. It was so beautiful. The only thing one could see in the room, alone on the table.'[15]

1946 Potters outside the Berkeley Gallery, London Left (standing) Lucie Rie, Sam Haile, William Ohly, (Berkeley Galleries) Laurie Cooke, Jean Smith, unknown, Patrick Heron, Bunty Smith, Kenneth Quick, Dorothy Kemp, Eileen Newton, Delia Heron, Jessamine Leach, Sylvia Fox Strangways, Harry Davis, Bernard Leach, unknown, Front. Dicon Nance, Dick Kendall, Frank Vibert, Margaret Leach, Mariel Cardew, Valerie Bond (white blouse), Horatio Dunn, Michael Leach. David Leach took the photograph

Wilhelmina Barns-Graham, a painter and friend of Bernard's for 37 years, in conversation with the author, remembers him as a true friend to all who knew him, 'So many people turned to him with their troubles. He listened to you as though you were the most important person in the world. People looked upon Bernard as a guru.' She first met him when he came to her Studio in St Ives and admired her work.

During the Festival of Britain in 1951 an exhibition - '15 Artists and Craftsmen from Around St Ives' - was organised by Denis Mitchell at the Mansard Gallery at Heals in Tottenham Court Road, London. The catalogue was printed by Guido Morris, who also exhibited his work, and the exhibitors were Bernard Leach, painters Ben Nicholson, Peter Lanyon, Patrick Heron, John Wells, Misome Peile, Bryan Wynter, Alfred Wallis, Terry Frost, Tom Early, W Barns-Graham, and sculptors Barbara Hepworth, Sven Berlin and Denis Mitchell. It was Leach who had first introduced Mitchell to Hepworth as someone who could handle material, having worked in Geevor tin mine. Denis assisted Barbara in her studio for ten years before buying a house and studio in Newlyn and establishing his own reputation as a sculptor.

Dartington International Conference 1952

Soetsu Yanagi, Bernard Leach and Shoji Hamada at Dartington, Devon 1952

In 1952 Bernard met up with his friends Hamada and Yanagi, representing Japan, at the Dartington Conference in Devon, an international gathering of potters and weavers to consider the role of the craftsman in the post-war period. It was the first of its kind and Lucie Rie, Hans Coper, Michael Cardew, Katharine Pleydell-Bouverie, Warren MacKenzie, Muriel Rose and many others associated with Leach attended. An exhibition featuring British craftsmen from 1920 to 1952 was organised and toured nationally.

Over a hundred delegates arrived from Europe, America, Asia and Africa to demonstrate and display their crafts, to lecture, and discuss their philosophies. One such lecture was given by Patrick Heron *Submerged Rhythm - A Potter's Aesthetic* in which he summed up the significance of the work of Bernard Leach and in the similarity of the potter and the painter in the creative act.

At the end of the conference Leach, Hamada and Yanagi,

at the invitation of the Society of Contemporary Arts in Washington, travelled across America, lecturing, demonstrating, exhibiting their work, talking about ceramics and the various aspects of arts and crafts recently raised at Dartington. The following year they toured Japan with a similar agenda. Willie Barns-Graham recalls: 'When Bernard was in Japan he sent letters on long yellow sheets of paper with drawings which we had to pass to a wide circle of friends.' Leach kept copious notes of his travels in Japan and in 1960 published a book recording his experiences *A Potter in Japan 1952-55*.

Janet Darnell at Mashiko

It was at Black Mountain College in America that sculptor and potter, Janet Darnell, met Leach and Hamada. The meeting changed her life. She was captured by Hamada's approach to potting and his easy flowing movements in throwing on the wheel. As her friendship with Bernard grew she asked him to recommend her as a student to Hamada. Hamada agreed. It was a major departure for Japan. At that time women were allowed to help in stacking the kilns and routine manual jobs, but not in actual pot making. Janet arrived in Japan in the spring of 1954.

Bernard and Janet Darnell (Leach) in Japan 1954

At Mashiko she found Hamada's family glazing and stacking his eight-chambered climbing kiln with Hamada surrounded by pots issuing instructions and decorating in rhythmic movements. She and Bernard were overawed by his deft handling of hundreds of pots which flowed through his hands. When Bernard asked how he did it he replied, 'I simply look at the pot and ask what it wants.'[16] His way of working was totally intuitive.

On the advice of Hamada, and after six months of travelling with him and Bernard visiting traditional pottery villages, Janet chose to work in the remote mountain village of Tamba, where pottery had been made for over one thousand years. She had not reckoned that she was of great news value. 'I had the mistaken idea that I was going to an isolated

Janet Darnell potting at Tamba, Japan 1954

area where I could work quietly in the prescribed study method of the East.'[17] Instead she found herself the first foreigner to work there and the only woman in Japan using the potter's wheel. Janet lived with the Ichino family, living a simple life, but enjoying the warmth and kindness extended to her, making pots and firing in the cave-like kilns. While she was working in Tamba, she would travel to Mashiko for Hamada's glazing and kiln firings and to listen to his advice.

Janet Leach runs the pottery

In 1956, after two years of intense study in Japan, where she felt she had fully realised herself as a potter, Janet came to England to marry Bernard. They set up house in the pottery cottage and Janet was immediately engaged in running the showroom, seeing visitors, organising the work load, as well as continuing to produce her own individual pieces. She believed in the standard-ware but declined to make it. Bernard was heavily committed to making pots for various international exhibitions.

Janet and Bernard dispensed with the apprenticeship system and engaged more advanced young potters from the art schools for a two-year period. 'We had four Americans, five Canadians, three New Zealanders, four Australians, three Indians, two French, one Belgian, a Dane and a goodly number of English.'[18] Bernard would select the students with a short trial period to judge their quality and potential. Janet bought a small house near the Barbara Hepworth workshops for the students so they could live their own lives and be free of restrictions.

Nirmala Patwardhan, secretary Joan and Bernard, in Barbara Hepworth's garden

The young potters were encouraged to produce individual pots, as well as developing their

skills in the necessary repetitious standard-ware, which paid their wages. It was a strict workshop discipline, but once acquired, was the foundation for their own success as potters. Janet and Bernard urged them to keep in mind that although the potter is making a hundred mugs, one person is going to buy and use one mug, and it must be the best that he or she can produce.

1963 Hamada's visit to the Leach Pottery. (left) Ian Steele, Warren MacKenzie, Mick Henry, unknown, unknown Shinsaku Hamada, Bernard, Shoji Hamada, Janet Leach, John Reeve, Glenn Lewis, Mirek Smisek, Jack Worseldine, unknown.

In the Leach Pottery Standard Ware Catalogue for 1970 Bernard wrote, 'I have been challenged as to why, after the Leach Pottery has been in existence for half a century, we still think that there is validity in producing and training the student-potters to make our standard catalogued ware. I firmly believe that no one can really teach anyone anything, but students may teach themselves by our words, example, good materials, throwing and firing techniques. Even today a standard of beauty and fine workmanship can emerge from a group, but the desire, the goodwill and the latency must be there.'

As demands on Bernard for his pots, for travels abroad, for lecturing, and for his writing increased, Bill Marshall gradually took over the supervision of standard-ware and helped Bernard by throwing some of his larger pots. The climbing kiln, which needed at least four experienced potters to fire it, was gradually abandoned and replaced with a smaller oil

1966 Hamada and wife visit the Leach Pottery. (left top) Trevor Corser, unknown, Jorgen Jorgensen, Susan Smith, Sylvia Hardaker, unknown, (front) John Reeve, Tony Burgess, Bernard, Bill Marshall, Shoji Hamada, Tim Stampton, Mrs Kazue Hamada and daughter, Janet Leach,

fired kiln. A separate kiln was built for the firing of experimental pots and the workshops were kept open in the evenings and weekends so that students could develop individual expression alongside their technical skills. After a successful firing Janet would provide a celebratory feast in the pottery. Bernard would discuss each piece with a highly critical eye and spared no one. He was a hard taskmaster, but one who also gave encouragement. High standard items were priced by Bernard and sold through the showroom or other suitable venues.

'Our records for 1970 show that we made over 15,000 pieces of standard-ware which varied in price from 14p to £2.50. I do not know the actual number of individual pots fired in the various kilns, but I estimate it to be between 4,000 and 5,000.' [18a]

Hamada and son Shinsaku at the Leach Pottery 1963

Bernard Leach retires from potting

With Janet to manage the pottery, Bernard was now free to continue to write books, visit Japan, concentrate on exhibiting and to receive many honours bestowed on him by this country and Japan. In 1974, with his eyesight failing, he gave up potting and eventually moved to a flat overlooking Porthmeor beach in St Ives, where he continued his writing by dictating into a tape recorder. He entertained artists and writers and many visitors, and continued to advise the students who came to the Leach Pottery to work by inviting them to tea at the flat at No.4 Barnaloft. His window overlooked the wild Atlantic ocean where surfers rode mountainous waves and high tide lapped the walls of the building. To his right was the Island with the little chapel of St Nicholas on its summit, decorated with a few Leach floor tiles. To the left Clodgy Point and Mans Head, outcrops of rocks which led to the wild moorland countryside known as West Penwith, and to the village of Zennor, six miles away. Bernard's poor vision did not diminish his appreciation of his immediate surroundings.

'When [semi] blindness hit him in January 1974, it did not depress him to the extent one would expect. To him it was almost a release and he was no longer divided trying to serve two worlds. He was now free from his dilemma and he could pursue his writing and religious activities without conflict. He rarely came to the Pottery because that depressed him; instead the potters visited him in the evenings. But I must say that up until a week before he died he occasionally said he had a dream of a pot that he wished he could have made before he lost his sight.'[19].

Mike Tooby, centre, first curator of Tate Gallery, St Ives, with Mashiko delegation to see exhibition of Leach and Hamada pots. (left) Toyonori Usuba, Tadashi Higets, Ikuzo Fujiware, Tomoo Hamada, Mizuki Oshikawa, Yoshihiro Yurugi, Professor Seiji Oshima, Nakaba Tsukamoto, Yoshihiro Otake, Heiya Tomita

Patrick Heron in his St Ives studio with Imi Arimoto, interpreter for Japanese delegation 1995

In 1977 a major retrospective exhibition was held at the Victoria and Albert Museum in honour of Bernard's ninetieth birthday. The display included 200 pots, with prints and drawings. The simple figurative motifs he used on his pots were the willow, the tree of life, bird, fish or hare, a leaf, various patterns and the human figure, usually against an Oriental background. All were loosely drawn with brush, comb, or tools he made himself from bamboo.

Many of Bernard's home-made tools are still in use at the Leach Pottery today.

A book *The Art of Bernard Leach* celebrating Bernard's ninetieth birthday, edited by Carol Hogben who, as curator, also organized his retrospective exhibition at the Victoria and Albert Museum, wrote – 'There is room, of course, for an infinite number of opinions as to who is the finest potter of our age, but there cannot be two views as to which has had the greatest influence on others.' Sadly, on Bernard's ninetieth birthday, his great friend, Shoji Hamada died. He had paid his last visit to St Ives in 1973.

David Leach with Tomoo Hamada, Dartington 1995, admiring a pot made by grandfather Shoji Hamada at Dartington in 1952

Tomoo Hamada at Leach fireplace, where his grandfather, Hamada, cooked his meals

Death of Bernard Leach

Bernard died in 1979. Alice Moore, known for her embroidery, recalled that fateful day. 'I was with Bernard when he died. It just happened. When I had a stroke he came to see me and I was very fond of him. When he was in hospital at Hayle I used to take him little tiny wild flowers from my garden because he liked to have them near him on his table, but he couldn't see them because he was blind. When he was dying Eleanor, his daughter, rang and said would I go and see him with her and pick some flowers from the garden. Bernard was lying on his back on a couch. We started talking about where we were born. All this talk stirred old memories for Bernard of his first wife and the early years, but very soon he became agitated and the nurse said she would get him to bed. Eleanor and I waited outside. Within a few minutes he had died.' Bernard is buried at Longstone Cemetary, Carbis Bay.

After Bernard's death Janet decided to concentrate on her own work, not to take students and to cease the production of standard-ware. A separate showroom was set aside for Bernard's work. Visitors travel from all over the world, especially Japan, to see where Bernard Leach and Shoji Hamada founded a pottery and an ideal way of working that built an enduring friendship and understanding between East and West. The Leach Pottery is the Mecca for masters, students, admirers and collectors of pottery. Paul Rice, in his book *British Studio Ceramics in the 20th Century*, wrote: 'A good number of excellent potters worked at St Ives. The mark they have left on the development of British studio ceramics cannot be erased.'

Early in 1995 the Nihon Mingeikan in Japan showed an exhibition entitled 'Bernard Leach and his Friends.' This same year ten delegates from the village of Mashiko visited Cornwall to view the Tate Gallery at St Ives and the Wingfield Digby collection of mainly Leach and Hamada pots; they were celebrating 75 years since Hamada's arrival in St Ives to establish the now famous pottery with Leach. Among the group was Tomoo, the son of Shinsaku and grandson of Hamada, carrying on the pottery tradition at Mashiko. While in St Ives Tomoo said the town was a place to fall in love with. When he returned in 2000 he said, 'I am delighted that someone with a passion to develop the Leach Pottery has taken it over. There has been a complete transformation which will be very good for St Ives and the relationship with Mashiko.'[19a]

***Right, back row**. David Leach, John Bedding, Ian Steele, Nic Harrison, Michael Cartwright, Trevor Corser, David Stannard, Tim Stampton. **Right, middle row**. Val Charalambous, Derek Emms, Robin Welch, Cecil Baugh, Ian Box, Bill Klock, Harry Isaacs. **Right, front row.** Author, Mary Gibson-Horrocks, Margaret Leach, Sylvia Hardaker, Janet Leach*

The Leach Legacy

In 1996 the author's first book on the pottery, *The Leach Legacy – St Ives Pottery and its Influence,* published by Redcliffe Press, Bristol, was launched at Tate Gallery St Ives.

Death of Janet Leach

With the passing of Janet Leach in 1997, the continuation of the pottery looked very much in doubt but the pottery was saved by Alan Gillam who, with the help of my list of potters from all over the world, began collecting pots to showcase in the converted cottage to interested visitors. Many of these potters also have work for sale in the showroom. David Leach, Lowerdown Pottery, with his son John of Muchelney Pottery, each brought work from their own potteries and expressed their delight at the transformation taking place at the Leach Pottery. Tomoo Hamada returned to St Ives in 2000, bringing his pots with him and promising pots from his family at Mashiko; his uncle, Atsuya, and his father, Shinsaku.

David Leach, Marion Whybrow, Janet Leach at Tate Gallery, St Ives, 1996 for the book launch and signing of The Leach Legacy : St Ives Pottery and its Influence

Death of David Leach

David Leach died in 2005. He was the last of the dynasty associated with the development of the Leach Pottery, although there remains his son John, who served his apprenticeship with his grandfather in the Leach workshops. He too has sons who are potters. John, Jeremy and Simon are doubtless aware of the responsibility they carry with the Leach name, although not directly connected with St Ives.

The future

The Leach Pottery has now entered another stage. In 2003, with the pottery up for sale, the Bernard Leach (St Ives) Trust was formed under the Chairmanship of Lady Carol Holland, to take in hand the caretaking of the pottery and to bring it into public ownership with major funding and the support of various public and private organisations. In 2005 the workshop was closed for major refurbishment. With the projected new plans and the proposed association with Falmouth School of Art and Tate St Ives, these major developments both recognise the Leach Pottery's historic and illustrious past, and will take it into the future.

Countless admirers of Bernard Leach and all he represented will look forward to the expected Leach Renaissance.

Discussion around the Leach fireplace with Bernard, centre. Right, Joe Benney, David Leach, Horatio Nelson Dunn, Kenneth Quick, Valerie Bond. Left, Frank Vibert, Mary Gibson Horrocks, Eileen Newton

Four Principals

Bernard Leach
Shoji Hamada
David Leach
Janet Leach

Bernard Howell Leach CBE

Born: Hong Kong 1887-1979
Studied: Slade School of Art & London School of Art
Leach Pottery: 1920-1979
Lived/worked in St Ives, Cornwall, UK

'Potting is one of the few activities today in which a person can use his natural faculties of head, heart, and hand in balance.'

Bernard Leach

Bernard Leach, the son of English parents, was born in Hong Kong, lived also in Japan and Singapore, until sent to Beaumont Jesuit School in Windsor, England, at the age of ten. In 1903 he entered the Slade School of Art and studied drawing under Henry Tonks. After an abortive attempt to work in a bank he returned to college to study etching under Frank Brangwyn at the London School of Art where, at the age of sixteen, he was the youngest student.

In 1909 he returned to Japan taking with him an etching press, and introducied the technique of etching into that culture. It was in Japan, at a raku party with his friend Soetsu Yanagi, that he decorated his first pot. When he held it in his hands he realised, 'I have got to do this.' In his article *'An English Artist in Japan in 1920'*, Yanagi stated that there are few people who are able to live in the spirit of Japan - Leach was such a man. He very successfully spanned two cultures and was the first artist educated in the West to learn the techniques of Oriental pottery.

Leach studied under the potter Ogata Kenzan with fellow pupil Kenkichi Tomimoto. Kenzan was sixth in line of a family of Master Potters dating back to the first Kenzan 1664 to 1773. Leach learned his 'alphabet

Vase, stoneware, Tree of Life motif

Bottle vase, porcelain

of clay' sitting on a hard floor, turning a Japanese potter's wheel with a stick. Leach and Tomimoto jointly inherited the title of Kenzan V11. A title, with the master's Densho (pottery glazes and recipes) was usually passed to a son, but being without a son Kenzan was happy to leave two pupils his title and techniques. With Kenzan's help in building a kiln Leach set up his first workshop in his garden.

In 1917 Leach was invited to build a pottery at Abiko, the home of Yanagi. It was here that Hamada wrote asking if he might meet Leach, whose pots he had admired while studying ceramics and glazing at technical college. Hamada desired to learn more of the art of potting and Leach required the technical ability of Hamada's experience of glazes. Leach, Hamada and Yanagi formed a lifelong friendship.

Bernard Leach revived the art of hand craft pottery which was traditional

in England before industrialisation. He spent his life learning what it meant to be a potter, and passed on his learning to his students. He encouraged prospective potters, by his teaching, influence, writing, and his philosophy. The Leach tradition in craftsmanship and aesthetics is spread world wide. Emmanuel Cooper expressed the view that Bernard Leach was the outstanding leader of the studio pottery movement.

Bernard said there was an appropriateness and relatedness in the parts of a pot, the foot, the belly, the neck, the shoulder. 'The form is the primary thing, texture, colour, pattern are secondary to the form, these are orchestration. The pot itself is the melody. The technique of learning to be a potter and to cover all the things involved, painting, sculpture, fine art, chemistry, geology, business, all these things are necessary. It's a very varied life.' [20] The decorative skills employed by Leach show a mastery of techniques through patterning of every kind, to figurative themes of various animal forms, to the willow tree and pilgrim plates.

Bottle, stoneware, tenmoku glaze

Earthenware Dish, Hare decoration

Among his many writings on ceramics, *A Potter's Book*, has been the most influential and inspirational. In the chapter 'Towards A Standard' he says, that 'pots, like all other forms of art, are human expressions: pleasure, pain or indifference before them depends upon their natures, and their natures are inevitably projections of the minds of their creators.'

Among many honours bestowed on Bernard Leach were in 1961, Honorary Doctorates in Literature from the University of Exeter and from Leeds University. One year later he was awarded the CBE. In Japan in 1966 he achieved the Order of the Sacred Treasure, second class, the highest award given to a foreigner. In 1968 he was granted Freedom of the Borough of St Ives in recognition of his international contribution to the arts. Barbara Hepworth and Ben Nicholson were also granted this honour (the latter was abroad and declined acceptance). In 1973 Leach was made a Companion of Honour.

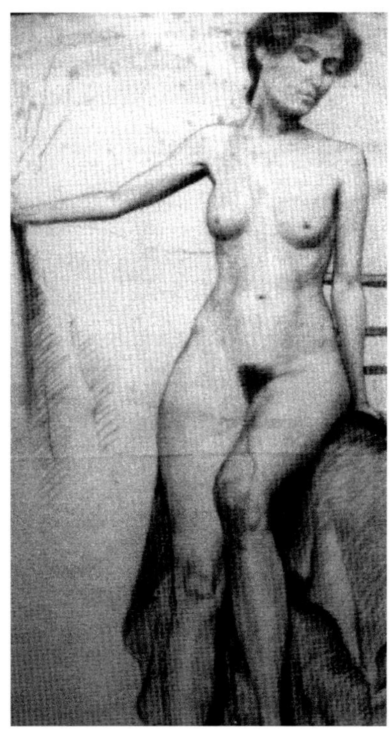

Bernard Leach 'My first drawing from the nude at the Slade 1903' signed BL

Leach and Hamada opening kiln at Mashiko 1934

Shoji Hamada

Born: Mizonokuchi, Kawasaki City, Tokyo
1894-1978
Studied: Tokyo Technical College
Leach Pottery: 1920-1923
Lived/worked in Mashiko, Japan

'I think my experience in St Ives was invaluable. No matter where you are, experience must come to you. To know I was on the other side of the earth had a special meaning.'

Shoji Hamada

Shoji Hamada was not born into a craftsman's household and had no tradition to copy. He therefore had freedom to embrace the crafts and pottery of Britain, using his knowledge of glaze chemistry learnt in Japan, and adopting the old traditions of English slipware. He was inspired by a small pitcher made by Leach and changed his studies from painting to ceramics. Their first meeting at Abiko, in Japan, grew into a lasting friendship. Shoji studied ceramics at Tokyo Technical College but felt his learning had very little to do with pottery techniques. He travelled to Cornwall with Bernard Leach in 1920 to set up the St Ives Pottery, building a Japanese three-chambered climbing kiln, the first to be installed in Britain. He also brought with him his traditional Japanese potter's wheel turned with a stick because he was not experienced in operating any other kind of wheel. In this small fishing town Hamada began his life's work.

In the early days of the pottery a great deal was lost in the firing, but they experimented and learned from their experiences. They also competed to see who could throw the biggest pot. By the time Hamada left St Ives many technical problems had been solved and he had held several exhibitions in London, the last in Bond Street, where he sold all but three pieces.

Bowl, stoneware with iron brush-work decoration

Vase, iron brushed leaf pattern

Hamada took up residence in the St Ives Pottery and built his bed from the same wood that was used to fire the kiln. It was the only timber available. The design was based on an Elizabethan four-poster bed at Pendeen Manor house in Cornwall. He also fell in love with English Windsor, and rush bottom chairs, and added many to his collection of furniture. After Hamada and Yanagi visited Britain in 1929, they returned to Japan 'richer by 300 chairs'. In 1974 Hamada commemorated his 80th birthday by donating his personal collection of paintings, glass, fabrics and objects from many countries, to the Mashiko Reference Collection Museum, which he founded for the benefit of the public.

When Hamada returned to Japan from St Ives in 1923 he set up his workshop at Mashiko in the company of rural potters. He was first attracted to the region by seeing a teapot made in that village, known today as Mingei, the folk craft village.

When he left Cornwall he also left behind his pottery seal and said, 'I now think it is unnecessary to put your seal or stamp on your work.' He believed that the identity of the artist should show itself in the work, reflecting the Japanese philosophy that beauty is related to humility. Hamada did not want people to judge a pot by a signature and was concerned with the 'good pot' not with his own personality. Many of his pieces are recognisable by his characteristic brush marks of a stem-leaf motif.

In Mashiko Hamada found natural clays with good plasticity and ash and stone for glazes. He worked with the simplest of materials, using hairs from local dogs for his brushes and practised a philosophy of producing first class work from impure natural materials. 'Mr Hamada feels that the good pot is the result of the naturalness and flow that come only from making many pots. It's like practising scales. If you make 50 pots, the last is apt to be the best.' [21]

Left: *Flower vase, sugar cane pattern*

Right: *Cut sided vase, tenmoko and rice ash glaze*

'Mashiko was a traditional pottery village. The potters made kitchen ware for Tokyo. Hamada transformed some of their traditional glazes such as Kaki into an art form. After the war Mashiko had hard times due to the introduction of plastic, and the sale of processed food. The potters, seeing Hamada on the hill, getting famous, began to do a Hamada-type domestic ware, and other potters moved into the area.' [22]

Many kilns have now been established in Mashiko and the village attracts numerous visitors. When Hamada, in 1975 was asked how he maintained his level of work he said: 'I feel now at my age my pots are better than when I was younger. Throwing, painting, pattern, all these techniques are quite natural to me and I can use them at will.'[23]

Hamada shaping pot on wheel

Shinsaku with Hamada, St Ives 1963

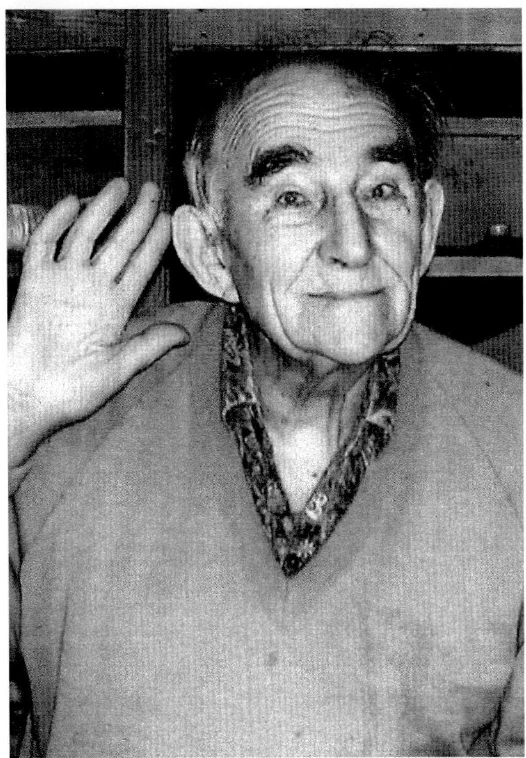

David Leach OBE

Born: Tokyo, Japan 1911-2005
Studied: North Staffs Technical College, Stoke on Trent
Leach Pottery: 1930-1955
Lived/worked in Bovey Tracey, Devon, UK

'My father's work and thinking were always in demand. I wanted to see his work which I loved, helped in any way I could. The team had its artistic director in Bernard. My own development could wait.'

David Leach

David Leach had his first pottery lessons as a boy from Hamada. At the age of 19, he joined his father at the Leach Pottery. There he realised a growing and instinctive appreciation of the unique importance of his father's work as an artist and of his need for support at the pottery on practical, and economic levels. In 1934 David, with the encouragement of the Elmhirsts, studied a three year technical and managerial course in the heart of the potteries. He applied these skills to developing standard-ware to practical and financial advantage.

He was not motivated by any personal creative need but acquired the necessary skills, learning from other students, such as Muriel Bell and Charlotte Epton, as well as from his father. In later years he benefited by example from Harry Davis who was an exceptionally skilled maker. In retrospect David recognises he was perhaps a little slow in not creating work on his own initiative, but he was never in conflict with his father's ideals nor felt any desire to remove himself from his influence. He enjoyed a fond working relationship with Bernard for 25 years.

In 1953 he was invited by the principal of Loughborough College of Art, Leicester, to head the Ceramics Department for a year. This forced

Bottle, stoneware, resist decoration

Teapot, porcelain, painted, foxglove

upon him a need to make decisions, both in his role as teacher and in reliance upon his own aesthetic judgment, which effectively made him more self sufficient.

In 1955 David relinquished his responsibilities with the Leach Pottery and moved with his family to Lowerdown Pottery, Bovey Tracey, Devon. It was time for him to have a life of his own, be his own master, and pass on his considerable knowledge. He was an inspired teacher and among his many students were his sons John, Jeremy and Simon. He made slipware for four years before changing to stoneware. David also developed delicate porcelain with hand carving, and pale green celadon glaze which the Sung dynasty Chinese potters likened to 'sky after rain.'

William A Ismay, a leading collector and critic, speaking at an exhibition of 'Three Generations of Leach' at the New Ashgate Gallery in 1986 said, 'His cut flutings on pots of essentially twentieth century feel are

among the most sensitive done by anyone since the technique was classically developed by oriental potters.' He was a meticulous potter, which is one reason for using porcelain. It is technically exacting to keep the shape of a delicate and semi-transparent object which has be to thrown carefully and thinly.

David was basically concerned with form made on the wheel in the first instance. His inspiration and thinking often came directly through working on the wheel with the clay flowing through his fingers. Right up to the end of his life he was still potting, had a showroom, and remained forever, an inspirational teacher. He was always keen to accept invitations to exhibit his work, to lecture

Jar, stoneware, floral motif, 24cm high

Dish, stoneware, willow tree pattern

and demonstrate. He travelled widely, assessed at various colleges, and was active in the Devon Guild of Craftsmen. He was awarded an OBE (Order of the British Empire) for services to ceramics in 1987. He was determined to maintain his interests and continue his life as a potter. He did this until only weeks before his death. He hoped, in his very full life, he would continue the things his father started - and get down to the written word. However, his biography has been written by Emmanuel Cooper so that partly relieved him of that responsibility.

At Lowerdown he made his own tools from metal, wood or bamboo, only teapot hole borers or drills were bought. He used both kick and power wheels. Of his work as a potter he said, 'I have studied and learned the drill of function so that I don't have to think about it any more. It does not occupy my conscious mind which is on qualitative things, shape, glaze, decoration.'

David Leach in his Lowerdown Pottery showroom 1994

David and Bernard on a visit to Dartington, 1977

Janet Leach

Born: Texas, USA 1918-1997
Studied: Inwood Pottery and Alfred University
Leach Pottery: 1956-1997
Lived/worked in St Ives, Cornwall, UK

'I didn't come to Cornwall as a student of Bernard's. I was a potter in my own right. I had my own ideas. I came to marry him .'

Janet Leach

Janet Leach (Darnell) as a young woman studied sculpture in New York. She worked as a sculptor's assistant on the Federal Art Project, set up to provide employment for artists, but it became obvious that a woman sculptor would run into difficulties trying to obtain commissions. During two years of the war she worked as a welder on naval warships, and afterwards studied ceramics at the Inwood Pottery and Alfred University. In 1947 she left New York City to start a pottery at Threefold Farm, Spring Valley, 25 miles north of the city where an artists'centre had been established for many years. At this time she was feeling dissatisfied with her work and defeated in her attempt to find the secret of making a good pot.

She became interested in the philosophy and techniques of Japanese pottery after meeting Bernard Leach, Shoji Hamada and Soetsu Yanagi at Black Mountain College, when they toured and lectured in America in 1952, immediately following the Dartington International Conference of Potters and Weavers. She was inspired by their commitment and love of the craft, and Hamada's flowing rhythms on the wheel, confirming his philosophy of simplicity and honesty. Through Bernard's introduction she received Hamada's permission to study with him in Japan for two years.

Left: *Pot with white pour decoration*

Right: *Slab pot, red clay, white pour glaze*

In 1954 Janet was the first foreign woman to study pottery in Japan, in Mashiko, and the only woman in Japan to be seen working on the potter's wheel. After six months in Mashiko Hamada advised her to study in the traditional country potteries. In the mountain village of Tamba, while living and working in the family pottery of Tanso Ichino, she did most of her serious potting. To return the favour, and hospitality provided by the kindly folk in the village of Tamba, in 1969 Janet invited Shigeyoshi, the son of the Ichino family, to work at the Leach pottery.

Making the most of her opportunities and experience Janet travelled widely, visiting the many folkcraft potteries, often with Hamada and Bernard. She met Bernard's friends, including Kenkichi Tomimoto and Kanjiro Kawai. During her stay in Japan she had the constant advice of Shoji Hamada and considered him her mentor. 'It was as a potter in Japan that I really started making decent pots. I think my pots matured in Japan.

I have done a lot of experiments in clay bodies. I like clay bodies rather than glazes.' Many of her pots are only slightly glazed. Janet came to Cornwall in 1956 to marry Bernard Leach. She found the stones, textures and granite walls very exciting and they had a great influence on her work. Bernard had a high regard for her individual style.

'I have always been an advocate of natural materials as much as possible, but I am not one of those who digs one's own clay. I think machinery has its place in our life as twentieth-century potters and I am pleased that our standard body

at the Leach Pottery is half natural "as dug" clay.' Janet's plea to the young potters of today was for a primary and simple approach to all the techniques involved in potting and advised that no amount of ingenious tools and mechanical knick-knacks would contribute to the making of a good pot.

Although she studied sculpture and pottery she never mixed the two 'each has its own standard.' Like many artists and craftsmen she could never imagine retiring. The lower room at the cottage was filled with pots which she admired, many of them made with the inspired hands of Shoji Hamada. A large 400 year old Tamba pot was placed so that it was the first object to meet her eye when she woke in the morning.

Janet in Kimono, Japan, 1954

Janet Leach in pottery cottage, with favourite pots, Barbara Hepworth sculpture and Kate Nicholson painting

Opposite top: *Vase, Bizen-style wood-fired, stoneware*

Opposite bottom: *Bizen-style wood-fired plate*

Colour Plates

Bernard Leach *Vase, leaping salmon*

Janet Leach *Large lugged vase*

Shoji Hamada *Bowl, stoneware, with brushwork patterns*

David Leach *Fluted jar, stoneware*

John Leach *Bottle, stoneware, wood-fired,wax resist decoration 23cm high*

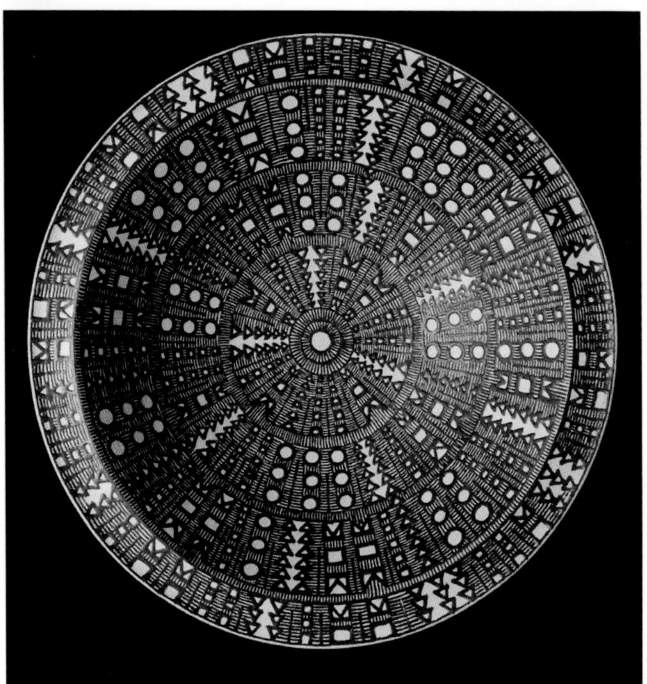

Valentinos Charalambous *Bowl, earthenware 52cm diameter*

Trevor Corser *Vase, stoneware, copper glazed*

John Bedding *Earthenware vessel, peacock pattern*

Shigeyoshi Ichino *Triangular bottle, wood-fired, stoneware*

William Marshall *Lidded jar, manganese chun glaze with white feldspar pours 28cm high*

Nirmala Patwardhan
Bowl, stoneware, with copper red glaze, 17.5cm diameter

Robin Welch
Vase, slab built stoneware

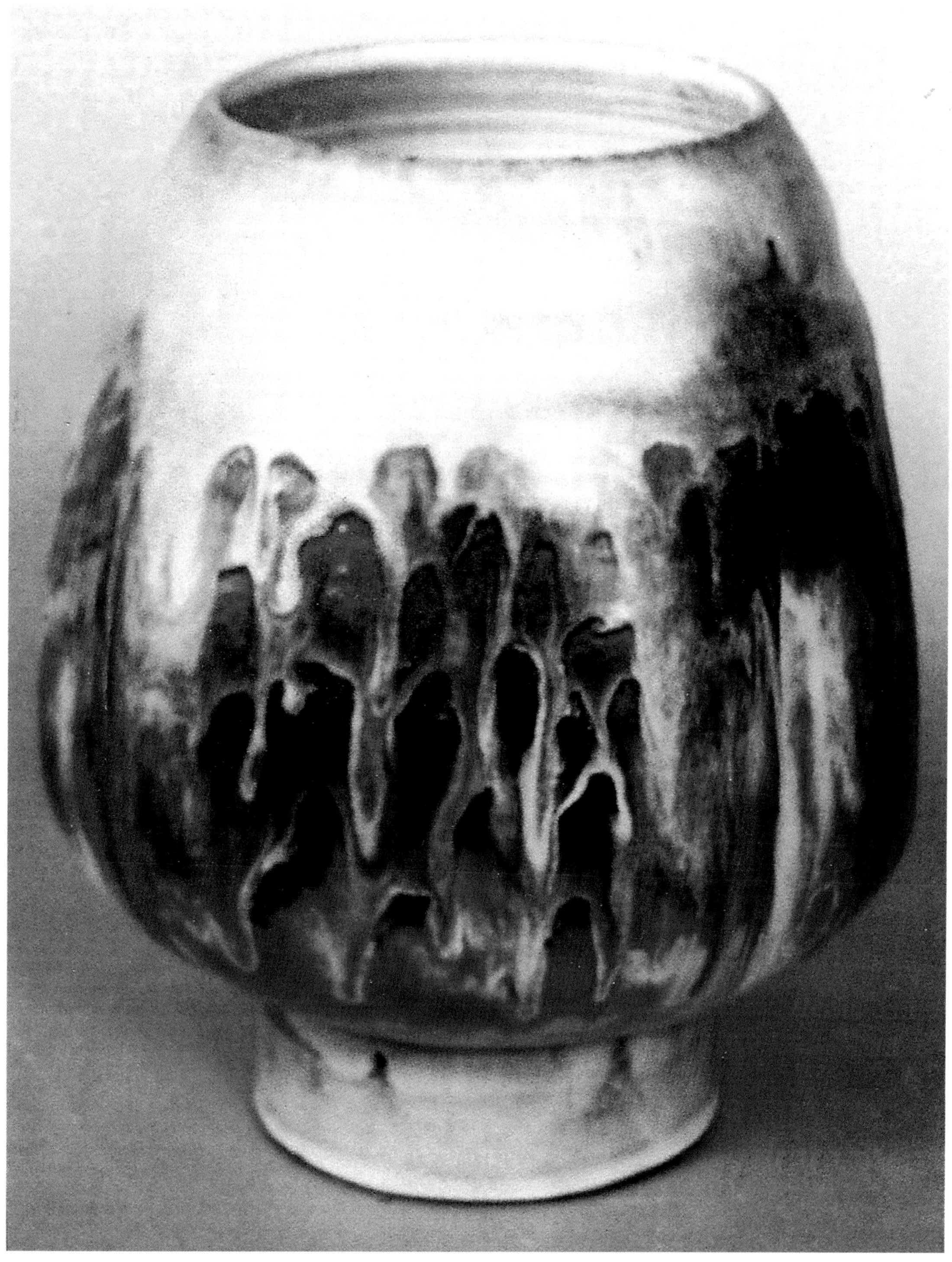

Cecil Baugh *Crater in clay earthenware*

Warren Mackenzie
Storage jar, stoneware 23cm high, 21cm diameter

Jason Wason
Vessel, 54cm diameter

William Klock
Vase, stamped impression on surface 75cm high

Richard Batterham
Covered caddy 15cm high

Gwyn Hanssen Pigott
Still life with yellow bowl, porcelain

Michael Cardew *Stem cup, stoneware, granite glaze with iron pigment decoration 12cm high*

Jeff Oestreich *Pedestal dish, soda fired, stoneware*

The Leach Potters

Michael Cardew CBE

Born: Wimbledon, Surrey 1901-1983
Studied: 'Greats' Oxford University
Leach Pottery: 1923-1926
Lived/worked in Bodmin, Cornwall, UK

'What I learned from Leach was the supreme importance of shape and how much depends upon the subtle differences of form, even in such apparently simple things as plates and dishes.'

Michael Cardew at Wenford Bridge

Michael Cardew shared with Leach a fascination for early English slipware. He was first introduced to traditional country pottery by W Fishley at Braunton, where he had learnt the rudimentaries of throwing. Having achieved this skill, he made his way to the Leach Pottery, where George Dunn handed him over to Hamada, who took him to see Bernard at the Count House , where they discovered a mutual admiration for English slipware. Michael first completed his studies at Oxford University then arrived at the Leach Pottery in 1923 to become Bernard's first student. The lessons he learned as a student at the St Ives Pottery helped build his personal philosophy. He was not interested in imitating the work of the master but acquired an aesthetic judgement that lasted a lifetime. 'There must have been a door marked 'Pottery' in my childhood.' [25]

He admired Hamada's pots and this influence was lasting. He thought Hamada was a magical man who made 'the most lovely raku out of red clay slipware', fired with raku glaze, red clay dipped in white, scragffito decoration with dashes of copper green.

His years at the Leach were very formative, especially conversations with Matsubayashi, Hamada and Norah Braden. He valued Bernard as a teacher,

Three storage jars, scraffito lettering 19cm high

who was able to articulate what Michael had always known but for which he couldn't find words.

In 1926 Michael bought a derelict pottery at Winchcombe in Gloucestershire and set up a rural workshop, reviving the English slipware tradition. In 1939 he left Winchcombe in the hands of Ray Finch, who had served an apprenticeship with him three years earlier, and moved to Cornwall where he set up the Wenford Bridge Pottery, near Bodmin, producing earthenware and stoneware.

Stoneware charger, Abuja 41.5cm diameter

Michael said of his hollow ware that he only ever made one pot and all that followed were variations of that one. These pieces were a vehicle for his vigorous brushwork or sgraffito decoration. His work was consistently at the English end between East and West.

In 1942-1948 he was pottery instructor at Achimota College in Ghana, following on from former St Ives students Kenneth Murray and Harry Davis. From 1951 to 1965 he worked in Ghana and Nigeria, introducing wheel-made pottery and stoneware to African pupils and developing his own range of work.

He returned to Wenford Bridge in 1965. His later years were spent making pots, writing, teaching and demonstrating. He toured America, Canada, Australia and New Zealand. His first book *Pioneer Pottery* was published in 1969. His autobiography was completed by his son Seth, who carried on the pottery for some time, marrying tradition with his own individual approach. Seth's son Ara is also a potter.

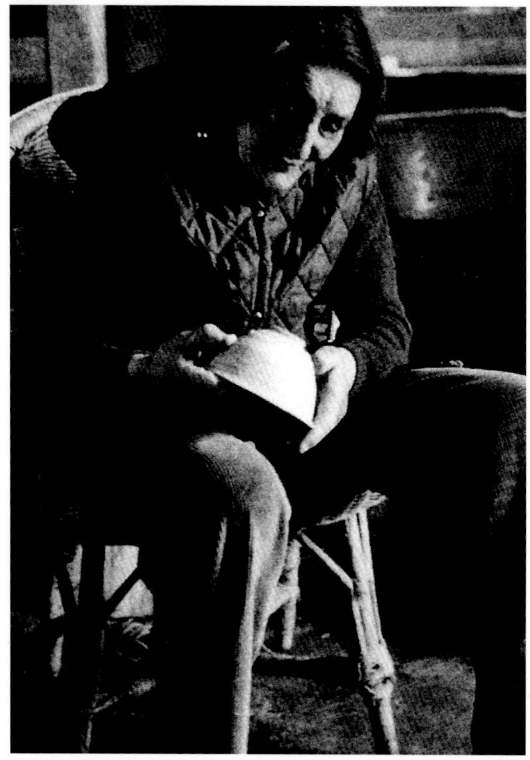

Katharine Pleydell-Bouverie

Born: Berkshire 1895-1985
Studied: Central School of Arts & Crafts
Leach Pottery: 1924-1925
Lived/worked in Wiltshire, UK

'It was a great experience and he was very kind, ungrudgingly generous with information and suggestions. He did not know the meaning of the words "trade secret"'

Katharine Pleydell-Bouverie

Katharine Pleydell-Bouverie or 'Beano' was influenced by the Omega Workshop pots of Roger Fry. After meeting Bernard Leach in London she joined him in St Ives, where she learned her craft in the company of Hamada and Matsubayashi. She saw their experiments with celadons, tenmoku, ash-glazed stoneware, and combed and trailed slipware pieces. Her year with Leach proved a turning point in her life. 'I have never known anyone who would give his time and attention so completely to another's problems.'[29] Before he left for Japan Matsubayashi made her a kick-wheel.

In 1925 she founded the Cole Pottery at Coleshill, Berkshire, in the grounds of the family estate, where Matsu designed her first kiln. She worked with Ada Mason and Norah Braden on a series of stoneware glaze tests which explored vegetable ash glazes made from plants and trees on her estate. Leach said her contribution had been important mainly in the use of matt-surfaced glazes in the composition of which the Oriental habit of using various wood ashes is normal. In writing *A Potter's Book* Leach asked her advice about ash glazes; he knew of no one who had looked into this procedure as thoroughly as she had.

Katharine Pleydell-Bouverie is now recognised as a pioneer in her

Celadon bowl

Celadon vase, stoneware

field, having devoted her long and active life to the study of ash glazes, diligently noting and registering each recipe. Many of her pots were designed to display flowers or plants. Sgraffito or combing were her favourite methods of decoration. Examples of her work, including her glaze recipes, are in the collection of the Holburne Museum, Bath.

In 1946 she bought Kilmington Manor in Wiltshire and set up a workshop in a barn once used as a maltings. Norah Braden worked with her each summer vacation. Katharine used both a Japanese wheel, which was spun by hand, and a treadle or kick wheel. She used five local clays; one - an ochre - had been in use since Roman times. In a letter to Bernard she wrote, 'I want my pots to make people think of things like pebbles and shells and birds' eggs and the stones over which moss grows.' [30]

Norah Braden

Born: 1901
Studied: Royal College of Art
Leach Pottery: 1924-1927
Lived in Sussex, UK

'Norah was perhaps the most sensitive of all the students who have spent time at the Pottery.' Bernard Leach

Norah Braden

Norah Braden studied painting at the Royal College of Art but switched to pottery under William Staite Murray. However, wanting to increase her knowledge and experience of studio pottery, she arrived at the Leach Pottery on the recommendation of Sir William Rothenstein, who said, 'I am sending you a genius,' She had been inspired by Leach's work which she saw exhibited in London and persuaded him to take her on as a student.

At first she acted as secretary, at a modest wage, ordering materials and arranging for pots to be packed and sent to exhibitions. She also agreed to work as an unpaid pottery assistant, to learn details of the craft of the potter, which she so eagerly desired to become. Norah Braden's contemporaries at that time were Michael Cardew and Katharine Pleydell-Bouverie.

The 1920s were an experimental era for the establishment of hand-crafted pots. It was also unusual at the time for a woman to take up such a craft. Bernard Leach was barely able to make a living from his tableware of individually made bowls, cups and plates. He relied on his more expensive studio pots, which he exhibited in London and Japan to provide an income. However, his three students flourished under his tuition.

Tea bowl, white glaze

Leach described Norah as one of the most gifted of potters. She was highly self-critical and because of Bernard's teaching of balance, the rim of the pot being right for the foot, and his belief in aesthetics, she became a hard judge of her efforts and destroyed much of her work. There is little evidence left of the pots she made in her time at the Leach Pottery although work is at Kettle's Yard, Cambridge and the Victoria and Albert Museum, London.

A firm friendship developed between Katharine Pleydell-Bouverie and Norah and in 1928, when Katharine set up a pottery on the family estate at Coleshill in Berkshire, Norah joined her. Together they worked on experimental glazes, using material gathered from the woods and surrounding countryside. They exhibited their work at the Little Gallery, London in 1929 and in Bond Street in 1930. The latter exhibition was singled out for praise in *The Times*, an achievement in itself. It was then unusual for potters to command critical acclaim.

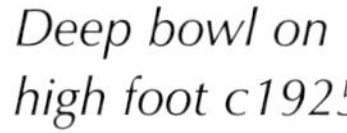

Deep bowl on high foot c1925

During school holidays she continued to work with Katharine at Kilmington Manor Pottery. In the 1950s Norah ceased potting. She taught at Brighton and Chichester Colleges of Art, Sussex, and at Camberwell School of Art, London. In 1994 her own collection of forty pots went on sale at Bonhams.

EP

Charlotte Epton

Born: Lincoln 1902-1970
Studied: Royal College of Art
Leach Pottery: 1927-1930
Lived/worked in Essex, UK

'The experience of working at the Leach Pottery meant a great deal to her.'
Richard Bawden

Charlotte Epton

Charlotte Epton attended the Royal College of Art, where she met her future husband, Edward Bawden, along with the painters Ben and Winifred Nicholson and sculptor, Henry Moore. She was studying painting and design whilst Edward was studying illustration and graphic design.

At St Ives Bernard encouraged her to produce work of her own design in the evenings. A disastrous fire at the Leach Pottery in 1931 destroyed much of her work and Charlotte left soon after. On leaving Leach she went to Cheltenham Ladies College to teach art. Michael Cardew was nearby at the Wincombe Pottery. They had both been students of Bernard Leach and a friendship developed which enabled Charlotte to renew her attachment to the art of pottery. Over a period she collected many of Michael's pots.

Her continued interest in pottery was furthered through working for Muriel Rose at The Little Gallery off Sloane Square in London. Muriel's shop was one of the first of its kind to sell hand-crafted pottery and remained open until the outbreak of war in 1939. Charlotte and Muriel had numerous discussions and arguments on the qualities of hand-thrown pottery. Muriel Rose's book *Artist Potters in England* was published by Faber in 1970.

When Charlotte married Edward Bawden in 1932 they moved to Essex, where her two children were born. The war intervened, Edward became an official war artist and Charlotte moved to Cheltenham for the safety of the children and taught as a senior art mistress at Pates Grammar School. After the war the family moved back to Essex where she was involved as an examiner in several art colleges. She was a member of Essex Education Committee, a magistrate and governor of several schools and also ran courses at Denman College.

Open vase, stoneware 9cm diameter

She began potting again with Joanna Constantinidis. Charlotte had a great 'feel' for pottery, its quality and style, and she has been described as a 'potter of subtlety and sensitivity.' The Victoria and Albert Museum purchased three of her pots. She believed in the philosophy of honesty and good design in hand-made pottery but also appreciated the English tradition of Wedgwood and commercial pottery.

Lidded pot, stoneware

Bernard Forrester

Born: Stoke-on-Trent 1908-1990
Studied: Apprenticeship with Minton Pottery
Leach Pottery: 1932-1934
Lived/worked at Bramble Moor Pottery, Devon, UK

'In 1932 Leach came to Dartington to establish the pottery at Shinners Bridge, and Bernard Forrester came with him to build the kiln.' David Winkley

Bernard Forrester

Bernard Forrester had already gained his skills as a modeller through his eight-year apprenticeship with the Minton Pottery, Stoke-on-Trent, and realised that production throwing held no interest for him. He had been persuaded to join the Leach Pottery by writer and critic Herbert Read when he was a painting student at Newcastle-under-Lyme, but even the small pottery at St Ives reminded him of his industrial experience He determined to make each pot a one off. Read also introduced him to the ceramic collection at the Victoria and Albert Museum, where he realised the endless possibilities of producing individual pieces.

In 1934 Bernard Forrester left the Leach Pottery to take over from David Leach at the new Dartington Pottery at Shinners Bridge, Devon, releasing David to study for a three year course on pottery management and ceramic technology, at North Staffordshire Polytechnic.

Bernard Forrester also ran a pottery course for adults locally, where he built the kiln and equipped the workshop. Combined with his teaching he made earthenware and stoneware, developing his style. He worked at Dartington Hall School for nearly forty years, enjoying a long working association with potter Marianne de Trey. At his funeral she said, 'there

Swooping bird vase, stoneware 16.5 cm high

Vase, stoneware, decorated with gold lustre 28 cm high

was something beyond the moral and social values that he had and beyond kindness and compassion which made him the remarkable man we all honour today.'

David Winkley, a member of the Devon Guild said of Bernard Forrester, 'It was he, who, with great generosity, encouraged me to start my first workshop, helped build my first kiln.' David had come to Dartington to teach drawing and history but watching Bernard throw changed the course of his life. Bernard Forrester was also a founder member of the Devon Guild of Craftsmen.

In 1952, his wife and partner, Helga, said they bought a house in Broadhempston, Devon, where he started Bramble Moor Pottery. He worked with lustre-fired porcelain in his final 25 years of potting. He was influenced by the jewel-like decorated pots of Persia and the brilliant colours and delicacy of gold tracery in the design. A retrospective exhibition was held at Dartington to celebrate his 80th birthday. Over a thousand people visited the exhibition to enjoy the work of someone who had brought so many students to an appreciation of pottery. His philosophy encouraged learning: 'There is so much to learn, experience and enjoy.'

Harry Davis

Born: Cardiff 1910-1986
***May Davis* 1914-1995**
Studied: Art
Leach Pottery: 1933-1937
Lived/worked mainly in Cornwall, UK

'Harry recognised the debt he owed Bernard for his introduction to Pottery. It was invaluable in learning to recognise the aesthetic qualities of a good pot.'
May Davis

Harry Davis

Harry Davis applied for the pottery class at art school but the classes were full. Undeterred he taught himself to pot after hours. It was discovered at the end-of-term firing that the largest pots, and greatest number, were those made by Harry. The principal was impressed and managed to get him a job in a local commercial pottery where he was taught to throw.

When the Elmhirsts asked Bernard Leach to set up a pottery at Dartington, he advertised for a thrower and Harry applied and got the job. However, this first attempt to establish a pottery at Dartington fell through and Bernard invited Harry to work with David at St Ives. Harry Davis proved to be a good organizer, as well as a skilful thrower, with an understanding of clays and glazes. He also helped in making the pottery a more commercial venture by devising methods and operations of various aspects of potting to work more efficiently.

At around the same time as Harry joined, a young paying student, May Scott, arrived to study for a year. She had spent a few months at a pottery in Malvern run by Muriel Bell, who had herself previously worked with Bernard. Harry taught May to throw. They married in 1937. Subsequently

Decorated tea cups and saucers

May set up a pottery in South Kensington, London and during the war worked with Michael Cardew at the Wenford Bridge Pottery in Cornwall, and also with Harry in Africa when he was teaching pottery at Achimota College on the Gold Coast.

Part coffee set, glazed light grey

After the war they converted Crowan Mill in Cornwall to a pottery, where they brought up a family and lived until 1962, after which they travelled to New Zealand and developed Crewenna Pottery where they continued their main form of decoration of brush work or wax resist, but increasingly Harry used incision, which was done on the freshly thrown pot. It was covered with fine horizontal lines and the pattern superimposed with broad strokes, using a piece of wood. Their pots were never signed but carried the workshop stamp.

In 1972 Harry and May started a rural pottery in Izcuchaco in the Peruvian Andes, to relieve poverty and help people achieve independence. This proved a testing ground for their ideas on producing pottery from basic local raw materials and making the machinery to process it. Harry made use of this experience on his return to New Zealand and wrote a book on making hand-made machines. Harry's advice was, 'Pottery is a valid and viable art-form in its own right, and potters should have the courage to be potters.'

D.Z.

Douglas Zadek

Born: London 1913-1990s
Studied: Bauhaus, Germany
Leach Pottery: 1936-1938
Lived in Cobham, Surrey, UK

'I liked Bernard's way of diagnosing a shape and analysing a curve. He had a Japanese approach to craft and admired the work of country potters.'

Douglas Zadek

Douglas Zadek returned to Britain in 1934 after the Bauhaus, in Germany, was closed down. He had studied ceramics and served an apprenticeship under Otto Lindig, who was the master potter at Weimar in Germany. He had lived with the Lindigs during the time of his studies. On first arriving in Britain Douglas got a job through Heals, the modern furniture store in Tottenham Court Road. It was in the potteries at Stoke-on-Trent and he hated it. He then worked for Muriel Bell, at her Malvern pottery. She had spent a brief period with Bernard in 1922 and at different times with David and Bernard Leach at Dartington, and with Margaret Leach at the Barn House Pottery in South Wales.

In London Douglas met Bernard in a gallery in Sloane Square, and liked his slipware pottery. Bernard asked him to come to St Ives. Harry and May Davis were leaving, to set up a pottery in South Kensington, and Douglas would be their replacement. He lived in the pottery cottage and struck up a friendship with Dicon Nance, who with his brother Robin, ran a furniture workshop in St Ives. They made many of the Leach wheels.

From 1947 to 1956 Douglas ran Surrey Pottery Limited with a partner, making slip colours, which were suddenly very popular and he was able

Vase, coffee pot, teapot

to employ seven people. Instead of using coloured glaze he made use of coloured slips as decoration. He then helped start the Craftsman Potters Association. At the Potters Croft in Oxshott he worked for Denise and Rosemary Wren, who were potting in the William Morris tradition.

Throughout his wide career Douglas had retained his interest in 'designing for a purpose,' a tradition which involved problem solving and came from his Bauhaus background and training. He was asked to design ash trays for British Airways, using their speed bird motif, and for Lawleys China and for the Royal Mail.

Douglas had kept in contact with the Leach family until Bernard died and had treasured his friendship. 'He was a fascinating and knowledgeable man to talk to. Although our background and philosophies involving pots were so different, it provided a subject for endless discussion.'

Two jugs

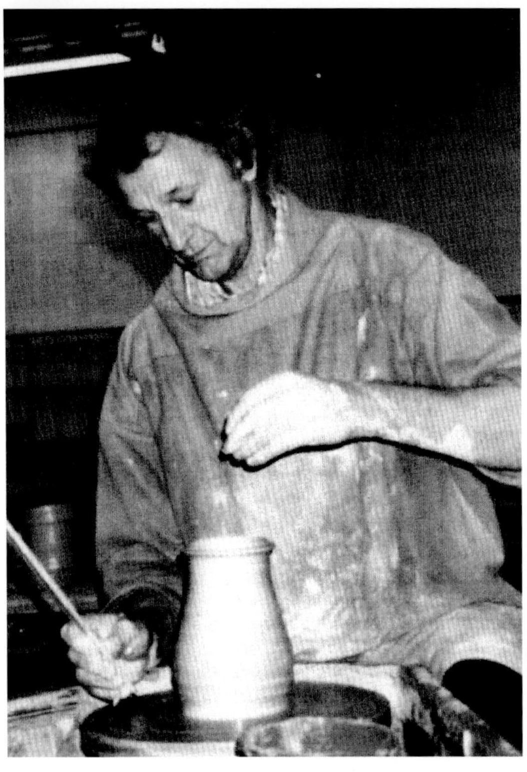

William Marshall

Born: St Ives, Cornwall 1923
Studied: First apprentice with Leach Pottery
Leach Pottery: 1938-1977
Lives/works in Lelant, Cornwall, UK

'Most of the critical training was delegated to either Bill Marshall or Kenneth Quick. We learned to see in the Leach manner which was a very critical viewing of all parts of the pot.' Warren MacKenzie

William Marshall

William Marshall was born in St Ives. He was the first apprentice to be taken on in 1938 by David Leach. He was 14 years of age and came straight from the local school. He trained and worked with David until 1955 and then with Bernard after David left to establish his own pottery in Devon. He worked at the Leach Pottery for 39 years, with a break during the Second World War when he was conscripted into the army in 1942 and returned in 1947. He was Bernard's hands, especially in the latter part of Leach's life, throwing the very large studio pots and leaving Bernard to detail the foot and rim, decorate and complete.

Bill Marshall is a superb thrower. He was foreman, senior craftsman and teacher to many of the students who passed through the Leach Pottery. These students invariably speak of his exemplary skills. As well as creating his own individual pots he had an extraordinary ability to interpret and carry out ideas. Leach would design pots and make drawings and Bill would translate those drawings into forms on the wheel.

In 1977 he set up his own pottery in the village of Lelant, near St Ives, making his own statements in expressive pots - 'one of the best in the country' - so stated Bernard Leach in *Beyond East and West*

Bowl with Hakeme brushed slip, decorated iron cobalt 19cm diameter

Faceted bottle, stoneware, nuka glaze with nuka copper pours 40cm high.

published in 1978, a year before he died. From 1955 when David left, Bill was his natural successor and worked closely with Bernard, discussing the various aspects of shape, size and style before Bill turned these abstract ideas into pots.

Together with his son Andrew, also a potter, Bill built a two-chambered wood and oil-fired kiln. As a lover of nature he draws his inspiration from the Cornish landscape, his colours and glazes from the natural effect of lichen on rocks, and the seasonal changes of plant life of the Penwith moors. Bill was also influenced by, and admired the philosophy, the skill, values and working ethic of Shoji Hamada.

As a person Bill is a reserved, stoic and matter-of-fact Cornishman, and to those who wish to write about him, or even pay tribute, he says, 'You may know that I have always preferred to work quietly and have always turned down such offers.' This does not deter tributes by craftsmen who served under him.

Dorothy Kemp

Born: Heaton Moor, Cheshire 1905-2001
Studied: Manchester University,
Honours History
Leach Pottery: 1939-1945
Lived in Felixstowe, Suffolk, UK

'Bernard helped me to appreciate good pots. I enjoyed the company of the team of interesting people and "Cornish Characters."'

Dorothy Kemp

Dorothy Kemp was teaching at Ecclesfield Grammar School, Sheffield, when she became interested in pottery as a hobby. Dora Billington, who taught ceramics at the Royal College of Art, London, and also held evening classes in technical training at the Central School of Art, advised her to go to the Leach Pottery as a student. Before the war Dorothy spent a few days with Bernard at Dartington, making slipware, and during the war she 'looked and learnt' in St Ives.

She became a life-long friend of Margaret Leach, who worked at the St Ives Pottery from 1942 to 1945. When Margaret left to set up The Barn Pottery in the Wye Valley, Gloucestershire, Dorothy transferred her working holiday visits to Margaret, continuing their friendship and enjoying the making of pots.

Dorothy particularly enjoyed seeing a studio pottery at work and making and firing good pots. She set up a workshop at home and also taught pottery. At this time the craft of ceramics was being introduced into schools and she taught it as part of the 'A' Level art course. Her book *English Slipware and How to Make It* was written for secondary school pupils, instructing them in techniques and standards in pottery. This was published by Faber in 1954 with a preface by Bernard Leach.

During the1950s the Victoria and Albert Museum, London, bought one of Dorothy Kemp's stoneware jugs, along with Bernard Leach, Michael Cardew, Harry Davis, and others they were acquiring at the time, to top up their representative collection of a diversity of pots and potters. They already had a range of pieces from the Leach Pottery and its successful students, who had branched out on their own, whether carrying on in the Leach tradition, or diversifying.

'I've not had my hands in clay for thirty years but I am still interested in the developments being made in studio pottery. I think Leach caused a sort of Renaissance in this field and his influence was great among his contemporaries. Then followed a reaction against this influence, to be followed by a still later generation of potters making good pots and original work.'

Jug

Pitcher

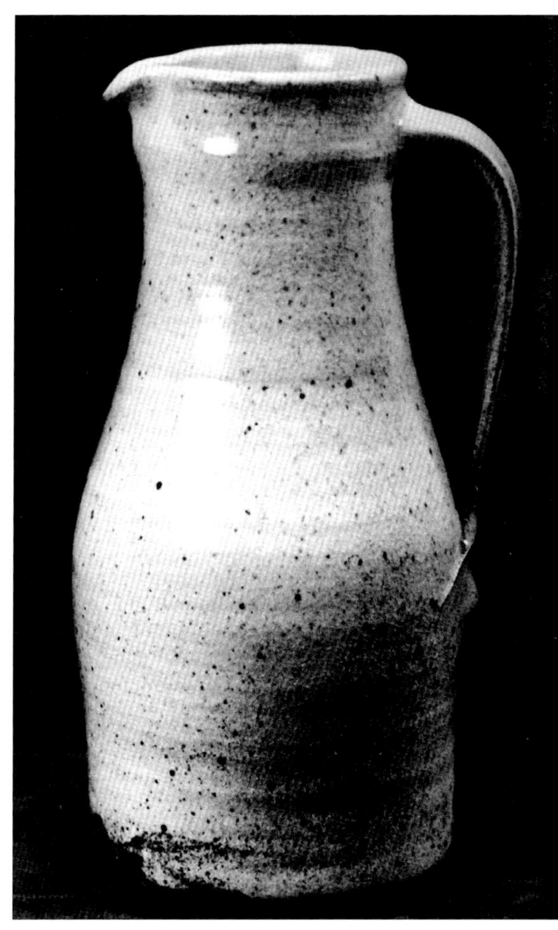

Margaret Leach

Born: Cheshire 1918-2003
Studied: Liverpool School of Art
Leach Pottery: 1941-1945
Lived in Ely, Cambridge, UK

'Bernard's insistence that pots are made to be used and that from using them daily one's perception is increased and refined, continues to be one of my principles.'

Margaret Leach

Margaret Leach (no relation) first became acquainted with the Leach Pottery when she spent two months of her summer vacation there while studying ceramics at Liverpool School of Art from 1936 to 1939. In 1941 she joined the pottery team, and was a competent thrower, glazer and adept at kiln firing, and soon making the standard ware. Margaret also grew vegetables in the pottery garden and found ingenious ways of cooking to eke out the meagre war-time rations.

Later personnel included Dick Kendall and Patrick Heron, who had been detailed to the pottery as conscientious objectors. They were joined by Aileen Newton. After four years, Margaret, who was regarded as a great asset to the running of the pottery, had to leave because her mother was ill, Valerie Bond (Prescott) took her place.

In 1946 Margaret took over the Barn Pottery in Brockweir, Gloucestershire. Her pottery seal was two Ws overlaid, standing for Wye Valley. She took on two or three students and worked in slipware until 1950 when the tenancy of the Barn ran out. One of the students, Lewis Groves, had started a small workshop about six miles away and she joined in that venture. 'Without the training I received from Bernard Leach, I could never have done all this.' She also remembers that all students at St Ives were gently warned, 'It takes twenty years to make a potter.'

She chose to work in slipware entirely and regarded this as her natural medium. Her pots were all red earthenware, with glazes ranging from dark brown/black to russet and golden yellow. Although the experience of firing to stoneware temperatures was useful she had no wish to move on to stoneware.

Jugs and plate, earthenware

The Leach teaching gave her an understanding and love of clay which she expressed as though she was still engaged in the craft, although she hadn't potted for many years. In 1994 she said, 'The love of clay is fortified by digging, weathering and preparing it. The relationship of body and glaze, jug and handle, or use of decoration is a subtlety that must be deeply felt.'

The final move to a community centre, at Upton-St-Leonards, where she worked for six years, completes her story. She married in 1956 and became Mrs Heron (not the painter Heron) and sadly, as with so many women artists, this ended her career as a potter. Several of her pieces are in the collection of the Victoria and Albert Museum.

Teapot, sugar bowl and jug, earthenware, slip decorated

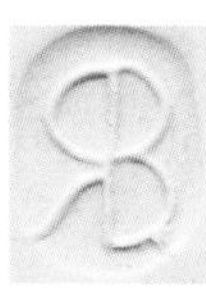

Robert Louis Blatherwick

Born: Lincoln 1920-1993
Studied: Trained at Wedgwood and Burslem Art School
Leach Pottery: 1942-1943
Lived/worked Lincoln, UK

'Bob often spoke of his time with Bernard Leach and admired him. He continued to work in his tradition and felt a pot was like a human body.' Marjorie Wheeldon

Robert Blatherwick

Robert Blatherwick received scholarships to attend Lincoln School of Art from the age of 12. Following his apprenticeship at Wedgwood, Stoke-on-Trent, he undertook further training at Winchcombe Pottery under the tuition of Michael Cardew and Ray Finch. Cardew recommended him to Bernard Leach. He went to St Ives Pottery where he assisted and was tutored by Bernard.

'Bob and I (Marjorie Blatherwick) went to see Bernard Leach before we were married. We talked of the future when we would set up a small pottery. Bernard warned us there would be difficulties. He was so right. He had overcome them in his own life and we did the same.'

During his working time at the Leach Robert met various visitors, Ethel Mairet the weaver, Ivan Mestrovic, sculptor, Sven Berlin, sculptor and painter, Gwen John and her brother Augustus. A particular friend was Dicon Nance who, with his brother Robin the furniture maker, established a workshop on the Wharf.

On an invitation from Lincoln School of Art to teach pottery and sculpture, Robert returned to his home town. He ran the pottery department from 1943 to 1967. When he gave up teaching he set up his

Earthenware coffee pot, teapot and jug

own pottery in Reepham, concentrating on high-fired earthenware. His wife Marjorie marketed and managed the showroom, bringing up three children entirely on the proceeds of the pottery. She said, 'Bob's aim was to produce pottery that was functional with aesthetic appeal.

Most of Robert's pots were earthenware, the body being a combination of two different clays that are balanced and strengthened by the addition of sand and grog, thereby aiding the throwing and firing processes. Coloured decoration was formed with slip, which was applied either by trailing, pouring or dripping. Other decorative effects were scratched or incised.

At a retrospective exhibition at the Usher Gallery, with the Lincolnshire Artists' Society in 1998, a former student, friend, artist and teacher, David Paton, paid tribute to his past tutor. 'Bob was a master craftsman – to watch him at work was both a privilege and inspiration. His sense of form and design were unerring and his influence on those he instructed profound.'

Many of Robert's pot were unsigned as he believed, as Hamada did, that a good pot spoke for itself regardless of the maker.

Earthenware vase with combed coloured slip

Michael Gill

Born: 1927
Studied: Princeton University, Chemistry
Leach Pottery: 1943
Lived in Sherborne, Dorset, UK

'I spent my summer holidays at the Leach Pottery with Bernard.'

Michael Gill

Michael Gill was introduced to pottery when he went to Bryanston School in Dorset. Donald Potter, the sculpture and metalwork teacher was his tutor. Potter had been an apprentice to Eric Gill and had spent some few months learning about pottery from Michael Cardew at Winchcombe.

The first Heals school exhibition was from Bryanston School, where the work was mostly that of Michael Gill as the senior potter. He had previously won the 'Old Boys' Prize for Extra Curricular Activities' with his pottery.

After reading chemistry at Princeton University he taught pottery for the Princeton Arts Group. 'One of my pupils was Albert Einstein's sister.' In 1949 he potted at the Central School of Art with Dora Billington and designed a twin-firebox wood-burning kiln. He spent a week potting with Lucie Rie, making mostly cups and saucers.

Michael then spent some years travelling, working in Copenhagen with Gutte Eriksen, helping with her glazes. He built kilns in Greece, Uganda and Tanganyike, and visited William Staite Murray in Rhodesia. In Johannesburg he developed stoneware and porcelain for Pat Cullinan at

Olifantsfontein studio run by Joan Methley, and held a one-man exhibition in Johannesburg in 1953. He visited Australia and New Zealand meeting and working with various potters, and during these years of travelling he also set up a pottery at Kibbutz Sasa in Israel.

From 1957 to 1966 he worked for the Uganda Development Corporation setting up pottery as a small industry. He built a teaching workshop and manufactured glazes and other materials. He built separate workshops for the successful students, and finally, built a centre that could sell the excess produce.

Nile centenary vase 30.5cm high

Michael returned to England to teach pottery for a few years and was then invited to run Izandla Pottery for the Transkei Development Corporation, a large workshop employing 18 women and 2 men. In 1986 he studied at Bristol University to do a PGCE in Chemistry with Maths subsidiary. He then taught Chemistry and physics. In 1990 he retired to manage 50 acres of family woodland and make pots.

'I am a great admirer of Bernard Leach, Michael Cardew, Harry Davis and Katharine Pleydell-Bouverie. I like the pottery of Ray Finch, Dick Batterham, Phil Rogers, Mike Dodd and Andrew Crouch. My ideal is thinly thrown high-fire reduced stoneware and impure porcelain with Eastern-type high alumina glazes containing phosphorus.'

In 2005 Michael Gill moved to Australia.

Bottle, white body glaze, brush design 24cm high 18cm diameter

Donald Mills

Born: Peckham, London 1922-1996
Studied: Central School of Arts and Crafts
Leach Pottery: Summer 1944
Lives/works in Chichester, Sussex, UK

'I was at the Leach Pottery for the summer of 1944. It was a holiday job, standing in for each person as they had time off.'

Donald Mills

Donald Mills was introduced to Pottery by Reginald Marlow at Croydon School of Art. He continued as a pottery student under Dora Billington, and stood in for her at the Central and at Kingston Schools of Art when she had a stroke. He then stayed on as technical assistant for a year. He met Bernard Leach during the war at the Arts and Crafts Society 19th Exhibition at the National Portrait Gallery in London, where they alternated daily in exhibitions of throwing. He was offered 'bed and board' and a stand-in job at the Leach Pottery, through a busy summer making standard ware. Following this he worked as a thrower at Fulham Pottery, London.

From 1945 to 1952 he was a full time potter, setting up the Donald Mills Pottery, near London Bridge with Eileen Lewenstein as a working partner from 1946 to 1948. They also employed some assistants. His wife Jacqueline joined him in 1948. She had studied drawing and painting at Willesden School of Art in London and was responsible for the painted decoration on the pots, which were sold to London stores like Heals, Peter Jones, Selfridges, and to America. 'We changed our style every two years so as not to soak the market.'

Donald was also involved in designing, producing and supplying a

Group of decorated pots

range of pottery equipment, which occupied much of his time for over twenty years, but in 1975 he and his wife returned to making pottery full time at Itchenor, near Chichester. They intended producing Lambeth Delft, but could not find a clean stoneware body ready prepared and, instead, found a porcelain used in making insulators. 'It took some time to learn how to use it because it is not very plastic but it can be worked very thinly. We try to make pots which people like better six months after they have bought them. It brings them back for more.'

He has exhibited widely and is represented by two pieces in the Victoria and Albert Museum collection. The Queen Mother purchased six stoneware mugs, from the Arts and Crafts Society 21st Exhibition at the Guildhall, London. Another mark of royal approval was the commission from Queen Elizabeth to make tankards as presents for the coachmen who drove the coach on her wedding day.

Decorated bowl

Mary Gibson Horrocks

Born: Kingston-on-Thames, Surrey 1923
Studied: Wimbledon School of Art
Leach Pottery: 1944-1947
Works in Buckfast Abbey, Devon UK

'Bernard Leach was very kind and patient with me because of my total deafness, nevertheless he was a firm and strict teacher.'

Mary Gibson Horrocks

Mary Gibson-Horrocks was sent to Bulmer Brickworks, Sudbury, Suffolk to start a pottery for the owner by her former teacher at Wimbledon, Robert W Baker. This was later taken over by Sam Haile. She had a burning ambition to work for Bernard Leach but at that time Leach did not encourage students straight from art school. Baker then arranged for her to go to Lake's Pottery at Truro to gain workshop experience.

After three months at Lake's she made an appointment to see Bernard and spent all day at St Ives having an interview and lunch. She then walked to Eagle's Nest for tea, the home of Arnold-Forster, landscape painter, and later the artist Patrick Heron, whom she met several times when he visited the Pottery. Other visitors she remembers were Barbara Hepworth, Ben Nicholson, and Sven Berlin, who was writing his book on the naive painter, Alfred Wallis. 'Lucie Rie would come down for weekends when she was making her buttons. I sat next to her.'

Mary had achieved her aim to work at the St Ives Pottery. She was engaged in throwing and glazing and was trained by Margaret Leach to pack the three-chambered climbing kiln. Margaret had served for three

Decorated tureen

Cheese dish

years and was leaving to set up the Barn Pottery at Brockweir, Gloucestershire. Mary helped Margaret to fire the first kiln at her new workshop.

In 1947 a business man called on Bernard looking for craftsmen to help him start a pottery in Surrey. She and Michael Cardew joined, followed by two African potters and Margaret Rey, a pupil of Staite Murray and Sam Haile. The venture was not successful. Michael Cardew returned to his pottery at Wenford Bridge, Cornwall, and Mary and Margaret Rey set up a workshop in the grounds of a girls' school; as well as teaching pottery they also made items for their shop in Oxford. In 1949 Mary joined Michael Cardew at Wenford Bridge. 'He was a good teacher and helped me tremendously.'

For a couple of years Mary worked with Alfred Ehlus at his pottery in Bovey Tracey which was bought by David Leach in 1955. After Alfred's death she moved to Buckfast Abbey and made tableware for the Abbey shop, as well as teaching the monks. She married in 1969 and became Boys-Adams. Buckfast Abbey continued to be her workshop, 'because it is so peaceful.'

Valerie Bond

Born: Croydon, Surrey 1923-2003
Studied: Bromley School of Art, Kent,
Royal College of Art, London
Leach Pottery: 1945-1946
Lived/worked in Bridport, Dorset, UK

'There really was a very good team spirit and Bernard was very kind. David was a very good and patient teacher.'

Valerie Bond

Valerie Bond arrived at the Leach Pottery in 1945 after a chance encounter with Mariel Cardew, wife of Michael, who gave her an introduction to Bernard. She spent four years as an art student at Bromley School of Art and worked on the land during the war. On her arrival at the pottery David Leach came out of the army, Horatio Dunn from the navy, and Kenneth Quick began work as an apprentice. On the staff were Aileen Newton, Mary Gibson-Horrocks and Margaret Leach.

The pottery team had their lists of shapes to make for the week and things went fairly smoothly, she recalls, except for panics at the time of exhibitions. 'In making the standard ware we had to have the shape exactly right, or it would be thrown away. Bernard drew each shape and we studied them before we made them. 'Handles had to "grow" like a tree, beakers had to "spring" and have an imaginary circle inside them, knobs had to be easy to "hold," feet were finished and turned at an angle to "flow" into the pots, and jugs had to "pour" well. It was satisfying to fill up one's board with pots and carry it away to put on the shelf.'

Enthusiasm for work and play was overwhelming; swimming, walking and cycling were part of the routine. At 11am everyone stopped for breakfast round the fire and Kenneth Quick made toast, spread with peanut butter. In the winter kneading had to be done outside and knuckles had permanent chilblains from the icy clay. 'In summer we often worked outside in the sun if we had "handling" to do, and felt very happy, with the Stennack bubbling by. There was a great deal of cheerful banter.'

In 1946 Valerie studied sculpture at the Royal College of Art under Frank Dobson and Paul Skeaping. Later she taught pottery at Camberwell School of Art, married, and became Mrs Prescott. At a studio in Kensington she began making shapes based on primitive birds of many different designs and was encouraged by Hans Coper, who saw them in the Berkeley Gallery. Photographs of them were exhibited in the Festival of Britain in London in 1951. For the last 25 years she engaged in creating wood engravings and drawings for The Countryman.

To celebrate Valerie's 50th anniversary of her first day at the Leach Pottery, John and Lizzie Leach held a firing at Muchelney Pottery in Somerset. Elizabeth and David Leach and friends came, and Valerie helped stoke the kiln.

Dish burnished with pebble

Kenneth Quick

Born: St Ives 1931-1963
Studied: Leach apprentice
Leach Pottery: 1945-55 & 1960-63
Lived/worked in St Ives, Cornwall, UK

'A desire to go to Japan and work with Hamada for a time developed, and, with this goal in mind, he saved up enough money for that purpose - we helped him.' [31]
Bernard Leach

Kenneth Quick

Kenneth Quick was one of the last of the Cornish apprentice potters taken on straight from the local school. He showed himself to be one of the most promising of the younger St Ives potters. He was a production thrower of standard ware but his work soon showed a distinct individuality, which is what Bernard Leach looked for in his students. He praised Kenneth's all-round capacity in the field of pottery. When Bernard saw a pot on a shelf that he approved of he would say, 'The character of the person who made that pot is coming through.'

When he was fully trained Kenneth taught many of the overseas students to throw. Two of the potters who worked with him were Alix and Warren MacKenzie who, although trained in an American art school, had yet to learn to make a shape from a specific amount of clay and to exercise critical judgement in the Leach tradition. Quick and the MacKenzies liked to experiment and develop their own techniques, hiring and firing the Leach kiln at weekends and working long hours into the evening perfecting their craft.

In 1955 Kenneth opened his own workshop, Tregenna Hill Pottery in St Ives, producing items for the kitchen and table, working in stoneware and red earthenware with his own seal signed KQ and or TH for the pottery. Kenneth exhibited and sold at Liberties, London. After five years of running a successful one-man venture he took a six months instruction and teaching post in America, at Haystack, a design centre and workshop in Maine.

On his return to Cornwall Kenneth asked Janet and Bernard if he could resume work at the Leach Pottery, to which they readily agreed. He and Bill Marshall (uncle of Kenneth) were mostly responsible for the training of the new influx of pottery students from art colleges, who were engaged on a two-year work-trainee basis.

After two further years of working at the St Ives Pottery, Bernard and Janet, anxious to encourage the young man in his further development and exploration of pottery, helped him to realise his ambition of going to Japan to study with Hamada. A month before coming home he was tragically drowned in a swimming accident. Bernard and Janet were devastated by the news.

Part coffee set, stoneware

Bowl

Gutte Eriksen

Born: Rodby in Lolland, Copenhagen Denmark 1918
Studied: Kunsthandvaerkeskolen, Copenhagen
Leach Pottery: 1948
Lives/works in Karlsminde, Denmark

'It is through Eriksen, who spent a short time with Bernard Leach in St Ives in the late forties, that Leach's voice has been heard most strongly in Denmark.' David Whiting

Gutte Eriksen

Gutte Eriksen set up her first studio with two other artists in Hareskov two years after completing her studies in Copenhagen. In 1942 she moved to her own studio in Kastrup and since 1953 she has worked in her present studio at Karlsminde. In 1948 she travelled to Cornwall and spent two months working with Bernard Leach at the St Ives Pottery.

Later the same year, extending her experience still further, she worked in France with Pierre Lion and Vassil Ivanoff. She taught at the Jutland Academy of Fine Arts, Aarhus, from 1968-71, 1973-74 and 1976-78. During these times she visited Japan to work with potters and study their methods and techniques. 'All this appears to have added up to a kind of world-view, in pots of great integrity. She has a deep respect for the materials she uses and gives them all the freedom she can. The pots fit into that Ruskinian definition of enriching art.' [26]

However, her pots are not marked by any particular tradition and are not derivative of the Leach mode but, as David Whiting wrote of her exhibition at Galerie Besson, in London, 'There is an understanding of the complexities and ambiguities of form - the object is not only about texture and colour, but also about assured drawing, and spatial relationships.'

Three large pots

Two bottles

Her pots vary in shape and size, very large and bold forms, dishes of different shapes, tall bottles, and a variety of poured and dipped glazes which, through repeated firings, become part of the body of the pot, rather than a form of decoration. Each wheel-thrown form is a new pot, an intuitive, yet mastered art of the potter in a creative performance with clay.

In 1972 Gutte Eriksen won the Gold Medal in Faenza and in 1985 was awarded the Thorvald Bindesboll Medal of the Danish Academy of Fine Arts. In 2000 Gutte was awarded the Prince Eugen Medal from the King of Sweden, and in 2003 was the Regis Master at the Northern Clay Centre in Minneapolis. In 2004 she was awarded the C F Hansen Medal from the Danish Academy of Fine Arts. She has exhibited widely and her work is in collections in various countries including, Scandinavia, Japan, USA, Scotland and in the Victoria and Albert Museum, London.

Cecil Baugh

Cecil Baugh

Born: Portland, Jamaica, West Indies
1908 -2005
Studied: Scholarship British Council
Leach Pottery: 1948-1950
Lives/works in Kingston, Jamaica

'My experience at the Leach Pottery was tremendous; it enabled me to take back to my home in Jamaica the potter's art in its true form.'

Cecil Baugh

Cecil Baugh, as a young man, was captivated by traditional African women potters who made low-fired earthenware pots. Having found his calling, he joined them age 17, learned their craft and worked as a potter until volunteering in 1941 to serve in the British Army. He served in North Africa and upon his return to Jamaica read of Bernard Leach's pottery in St Ives. Awarded a British Council Scholarship for 1949, Baugh was impatient to begin his studies and came to Britain in 1948 aboard the SS Empire Windrush, carrying the first post-1945 Caribbean migrants to the UK.

In England he studied pottery with Margaret Leach at the Barn Pottery, a former student of Bernard's, and was then accepted at the Leach Pottery. He also visited Stoke-on-Trent to experience mass production wares, met Michael Cardew and helped to solve problems of porous clay with David Leach. While at Dartington Pottery he demonstrated the Jamaican walk-around free-form technique, repeated for BBC television in 1949. Baugh returned home and built a studio in Kingston and held his first one-man exhibition in 1950. A stoneware pot made at the Leach Pottery exposed a new technique. He subsequently shared that technical knowledge with fellow potters in Jamaica.

Together with sculptor Edna Manley, painter Albert Huie, graphic artist Lyndon Leslie and woodworker Jerry Isaacs, Baugh founded in 1950 The Arts and Craft School in Jamaica, which ultimately became the Edna Manley College of the Visual and Performing Arts, where he was head of Ceramics until his retirement in 1974, influencing generations of potters. In retirement he continued research on the use of local materials in glazes.

A Looping Syndrome stoneware, reduction fired

Cecil Baugh's works have been presented to the Queen of England (she now has four of his pots), the Emperor of Japan, Pope John Paul the Second and President Nelson Mandela, among others. He served on the Board of the National Gallery of Jamaica from 1984-1998 and was awarded the Gold Musgrave Medal in 1984 'for distinguished eminence in the field of ceramics.' The book, Baugh: *Jamaica's Master Potter* written in 1986 with Laura Tanna, covers his life and art. The 1999 edition, inspired by Marion Whybrow's book *The Leach Legacy – St Ives Pottery and its Influence* includes a chapter on Jamaican potters Baugh has influenced. In 2003 the Government bestowed the Order of Jamaica upon him and in 2004 he received The Gleaner Honour Award for Excellence in Arts and Culture.

Bottle vase, stoneware 34cm high

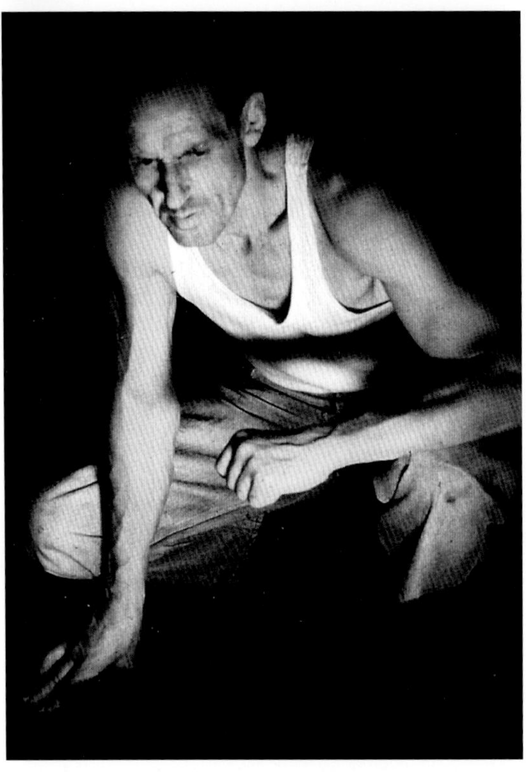

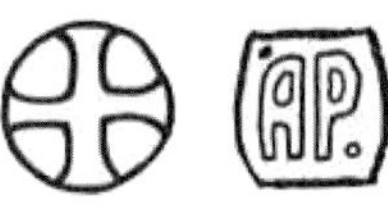

Geoffrey Whiting

Born: Stocksfield, Northumberland
1919-1988
Studied: Birmingham School of Architecture
Leach Pottery: 1949
Lived/worked in Canterbury, Kent, UK

'Although we have not had much contact your work is closer to ours than anybodys.' [32]
Bernard Leach

Geoffrey Whiting

Geoffrey Whiting was a disciple of Leach. On his return from India as a young man, where he made pots with the 'untouchables', he discovered *A Potter's Book*. It accorded with his interest in Eastern ideas, and gave his life a new purpose. It was also a practical manual and an aid in developing his pottery workshop. He visited Bernard in 1949 and regularly over the next 20 years.

His first pottery was at Stoke Prior, near Bromsgrove. In 1955 he established Avoncroft Pottery at Hampton Lovett, Worcestershire which Bernard visited on several occasions. Bernard wrote a foreword for the catalogue of his 1960 exhibition in Worcester. Geoffrey was impressed by the idea of several potters working together as a team and created an apprenticeship system like the one he admired at St Ives. He believed in the value of repetitive throwing in developing technical ability, and encouraged a workshop rhythm and discipline. He has been described as a 'pyromantic,' one in love with the art of firing and its creative results. He designed a two chambered kiln based on the Leach climbing kiln and fired with wood and coal.

His early pots were influenced by Leach but he developed an assured style of his own. Geoffrey was inspired by English Mediaeval pots and the

Bowl, fish decorated

ceramic traditions of Korea, China and Japan. Individual work was never a priority over standard ware and domestic pots for the table. Bernard thought Geoffrey's teapots the best in England and acquired one for his own collection. Bernard wrote, 'I would like to say how very good I think your article was in the last number of Pottery Quarterly. Almost everything that had to be said, you said about teapots.' [33] Geoffrey's teapots were chosen for exhibition at the Design Centre, London.

In 1972 he became potter-in-residence at St Augustine's College, Canterbury, where he combined teaching and pottery making and established a teaching workshop for King's School, Canterbury. In 1976 he shared an exhibition with the painter Duncan Grant at Lewes, Sussex, and was represented in The Leach Tradition at the Craftsman Potters Association in 1987 and in Galerie Besson, London.

Tea bowl, decorated

Warren Mackenzie

Warren MacKenzie
Born: Kansas City, Missouri, 1924
Alix MacKenzie
Born: Chicago, 1922-1962
Studied: Art Institute of Chicago
Leach Pottery: 1949-1952
Lives/works in Minnesota, USA

'Bernard Leach was the most important influence on my life that ever was. I know that his example as a person of conviction and integrity showed me how to live.

Warren Mackenzie

Warren MacKenzie and his wife Alix lived for two years in the pottery cottage at St Ives with Bernard Leach and learned much of value from their conversations with him. 'He taught me to see, to think and to feel. Nothing is as important as those things.'

Although Warren and Alix had studied at an American art school they found the training in ceramics inadequate. However, Bernard saw some potential in them and after nearly a year they developed competence in throwing and producing standard ware. Anxious to experiment and develop their own ideas they worked weekends and evenings building up a collection of pots and hiring space in the kiln for firing, which they had helped David to rebuild.

In 1952 the MacKenzies returned to America. On their lecture and demonstration tour of the States Leach, Hamada and Yanagi, stayed with the MacKenzies, who had also smoothed the way for their tour. A year later Warren was appointed lecturer at the University of Minnesota, which ran parallel with his career as a potter. They acquired a farmhouse with a workshop at Stillwater and built a two-chambered climbing kiln. Alix decorated most of the pots. She also threw. She used decoration to bring

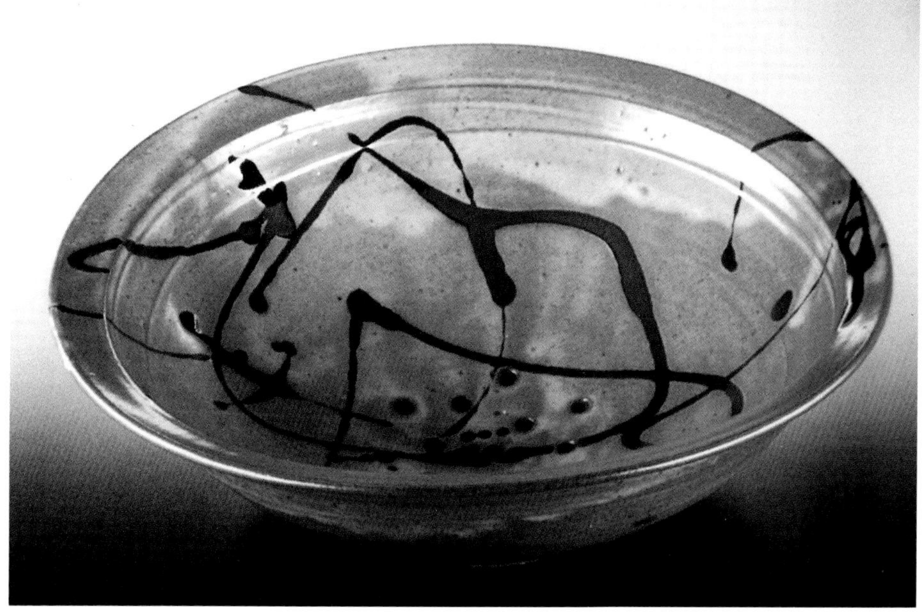

Colandar or steamer, stoneware 36cm wide, 14cm deep

Vase, stoneware 28cm high

out the individual character of the pot. After Alix's death Warren concentrated on form, surface, texture and colour.

Warren uses an adaptation of the wheel originally built for the St Ives Pottery by Dicon Nance, a local furniture maker. The use of a large kiln and reduction firing encourages the unexpected. He thinks functional pottery is the higher form of art, the 'real point' being that they are designed to be handled. 'My pots are utilitarian pots that people can use in their homes and this is a direct result of my contact with Bernard. He is convinced that without Bernard's pioneering leadership pottery made by the individual craftsman would not have realised the acclaim it enjoys today.

Every potter decides what his ideals are and for MacKenzie the emphasis is clear: 'I am a potter; a maker of containers and useful objects. The repetition of form and ideas over months and even years allows them to sink into the subconscious and to surface again, transmuted by changes in myself and in my environment.'

Valentinos Charalambous

Born: Famagusta, Cyprus 1929
Studied: Central School of Arts and Crafts, London
Leach Pottery: 1950-1951
Lives/works in Limassol and Nicosia

'My work isn't directly influenced by Bernard Leach but life is much richer for having known him. Even now, I find myself asking "what would BL have thought of this?"

Valentinos Charalambous

Valentinos was born into a family of traditional potters. To broaden his horizons, he studied under Dora Billington and Gilbert Harding-Green at the Central School in 1948. Leach's *A Potter's Book* was the 'Bible' and everyone's ambition was to work with the master. Valentinos wrote, giving his family credentials. Bernard replied: "Come down. You are a potter's son, and one cannot be a potter without having the taste of clay as a young man."

Along with other acolytes, Valentinos threw domestic pots to Bernard Leach's designs, but enjoyed a free day each week to create his own work. At the evening gatherings, 'Leach showed great humility, listening as well as talking, treating us as his equals.' But he was a stern judge and never held back in his comments.

Back in Cyprus, Valentinos immersed himself in his national culture. 'Bernard represented understatement; in the middle East, we overstate.' The family had borrowed to send Valentinos to London and to repay the bank, he was forced to produce and sell commercial work - mainly to British service families on the island.

Artistic salvation was round the corner. Valentinos was invited by the

Iraqi Ministry of Education to establish a Department of Ceramics at the Institute of Fine Arts in Baghdad. His life's work in the Middle East and Cyprus has meant that his own creative work could develop with integrity.

A major one-man exhibition in Nicosia in April 1996 confirmed Valentinos' stature as a master artist. The work on show was redolent of the traditions of Greek and Middle East ceramics, with decorated bowls and dishes alongside huge ceramic sculptures. 'My work, whether ceramic sculpture, murals, or simple domestic ware, is the synthesis of emotion, artistic experiences, and exposure to other cultures over many years.'

Dora Billington wrote, 'Valentinos' individuality and unwillingness to go along with the international stream is truly of value today, when contemporary idioms in all the arts are inclined to be the same the world over.'

Since the late nineties he has been carrying out extensive experiments on a mineral called Glauconite or Celadonite. He extracts this mineral from the land near his house on the mountains, where he lives. He believes this mineral has not been used in ceramics before. His experiments have yielded a variety of exciting results and a large range of colours, both at earthenware and stoneware temperatures.

From 2000 onwards he has received a number of awards from the International Biographical Centre of Cambridge, as well as by the American Biographical Institute. Amongst them a Lifetime Achievement Award.

Left: *Bowl, earthenware with foot 35cm high 48cm diameter*

Right: *Bottle, earthenware 45cm high*

Michael Leach

Born: Tokyo, Japan 1913-1985
Studied: Cambridge University, Natural Science
Leach Pottery: 1950-1955
Lived/worked in Yelland, Devon, UK

'Michael derived a lot from his father. He seemed to assimilate the ideas of Bernard and like him always made the best he could from what was available in nature.' Myra Leach

Michael Leach

Michael Leach, second son of Bernard, had an early introduction to his father's pottery, where he came every afternoon as a nine-year old boy and was fortunate to know Shoji Hamada and Matsubayashi, also Bernard's first students Michael Cardew and Katharine Pleydell-Bouverie. In 1927 with some help from his father and his science teacher, he was able to establish a small pottery at his school. In 1939 after university, and teaching biology, he decided to pursue ceramics as a vocation.

He met his wife in East Africa during the war. He was released from military duties there in order to build two potteries, the first in Kenya, the other in Uganda. They produced mugs and useful items for the troops but after the war they returned to England to work in the potteries at Stoke-on-Trent. On hearing that David Leach was vacating his post of teaching pottery at Penzance School of Art, Michael stepped into his shoes. He also worked for his father at the Leach Pottery and shared the running of it while Bernard was in Japan and David at Loughborough College.

In 1950 Michael joined David and Bernard at the Leach Pottery, but in 1955 he left to strike out on his own. He moved to North Devon, bought a farmhouse and converted it into the Yelland Pottery, where he and his wife

Slipware dish

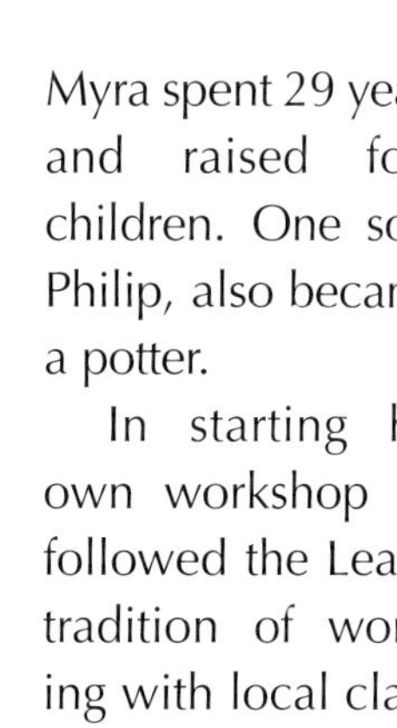

Myra spent 29 years and raised four children. One son, Philip, also became a potter.

In starting his own workshop he followed the Leach tradition of working with local clays and mixing the clay by hand. The Devon clays were ideal material. He used very little mechanical aids having just one electric wheel, the others were kick wheels. His first batch of pots were in earthenware but he changed to stoneware, making domestic articles for the table and decorative individual pieces. His pots were the natural colours of browns, greens and greys and a wood ash for glaze bought from a local farm.

Like his father and brother, he trained many potters and always had students. He carried on the ideas of the Leach Pottery in keeping to the basics and training his students to observe the fundamentals of nature in the making of pots. In 1995 a Memorial Exhibition was held at the North Devon Museum in Barnstaple.

Slipware dish

SM

Scott Marshall

Born: St Ives, Cornwall 1936
Studied: Leach apprentice
Leach Pottery: 1951-1961
Lives/works in St Just, Cornwall, UK

' The experience gained at the Leach Pottery gave me a good all round training and basically I am continuing that knowledge in my own work.'

Scott Marshall

Scott Marshall was the last of the apprentice potters to work at the Leach Pottery. As a young man he lived close by and often visited the workshop and watched his uncle, Bill Marshall, at his work. It was a natural progression from leaving school to be taken on as an apprentice.

Although he had no art school background he gained his knowledge from five years' experience in a working environment. He received his training from Bill and Kenneth Quick and from everyone else who was working there, especially David and Michael Leach. 'Bernard was at this time largely creating his own work, but was around to criticise the pots being produced and to ensure the maintenance of quality.'

During his five-year apprenticeship Scott learnt to throw pots to a precise size and weight and to produce a repetition of bowls, mugs, plates and a variety of domestic items, often working from a drawing or photograph. 'I have carried on in the same tradition because I enjoy making pots which have a useful purpose.'

In 1961 he started the Boscean Pottery at St Just in Cornwall, in partnership with Richard Jenkins, and created a small workshop, where they took on a few apprentices through the 1960s and 1970s. They built

Showroom of standard ware pots

a large oil fired kiln, similar to the Leach Japanese climbing kiln, which used to hold 1500 pots. Since the death of his partner Scott has worked on his own, but with support and additional help from his wife, Beth.

He still makes a variety of domestic pots in stoneware for the oven, kitchen and table. He uses an electric kiln and obtains 'reasonable results' from wood ash glazes with a combination of other additives to provide variation. He likes having direct contact with the person buying his pottery, especially neighbours and local people, and moves naturally between his workshop and showroom to provide a personal service. The pleasure he gains and gives through the making of pots, and the appreciation he receives, is the reward for a lifetime in his chosen way of living.

Lustre pots

David Stannard

Born: Berkeley, California USA 1925
Studied: Universities of Redlands and Oregon
Leach Pottery: 1952-1953
Lives/works in Alaska, USA

'I went to the Leach Pottery because I'd read A Potter's Book. His views of the unpretentious origins of good work resonated with my childhood memories.'

David Stannard

David Stannard, although born in America, was taken to China at the age of four. 'I grew up in an iron-age crafts-economics society. Raised in this tidewater of cultural diversity I returned to the United States with a preference for rural self-sufficiency, where materials which are needed are developed locally rather than imported.' He studied chemistry, biology and the science of soils. With this experience he pursued his interest in the craft of pottery and began work at Tacket Associates, a small pottery in the Los Angeles area that produced quality earthenware. He was responsible for clay and glaze preparation, casting, glazing and firing. Some time later he joined a village of potters at La Otumba in Mexico.

To further his interest he required more experience in an operating pottery. 'I needed a personal place to stand and face society.' After writing to Bernard he was invited to be part of the team at St Ives. Bernard wrote, 'So much of your beginning is akin to my own that I cannot help feeling that this would probably be the best place for you to come.' After a short time he began throwing acceptable pots and spent the year as a thrower producing standard ware. During his time in Cornwall he worked for two months at the Wenford Bridge Pottery with Michael Cardew and an

Australian potter Ivan McMeekin, and realised two successful firings.

On returning to America he set up Hill Top Stoneware, Oregon, using local resources and ran it from 1954 to 1978. Alongside he taught Basic Design and Ceramics at the University of Oregon from 1965 to 1980 and researched the mineral composition of Chinese and Western porcelain stones. His present home and workshop is Local Buoyancy. His quality of life is summed up in his philosophy of 'prospecting. processing, producing, and adding human value to local resources for a sustainable future.' He produces pots which carry the memory of their origins in the nearby countryside.

Pitcher, Indian Creek stoneware. Goblet, Oregon porcelain stone

'I find it almost impossible to tell you anything about my pots - except to caution that you need to put them to use, wave them about, examine them in the sunlight, scrub them at the sink, to form a personal opinion.'

Covered pot, Indian Creek stoneware, with two bowls

RW

Robin Welch

Born: Nuneaton, Warwickshire 1936
Studied: Penzance School of Art, Central School of Art, London
Leach Pottery: 1953
Lives/works in Eye, Suffolk, UK

'I can still see, feel, and smell, the atmosphere in that workshop to this day. It was an experience I shall never forget.'

Robin Welch

Robin Welch has worked widely within ceramics but has always returned to making one-off pieces. This has been central to his life as a potter. Vase and bowl forms of varying scale and shape have been the constant in his output of individual pots. He experiments with materials on surface decoration, introducing colour with enamels and lustres in mostly abstract designs. His large forms are both thrown and hand-built to bring them to the desired height or shape.

Complementing, and often used as background to his pots, are his paintings, which are a reflection of his forms and in their abstraction closely related to the decorative aspect of the pottery. The combination of the two is powerful and evocative.

He first met Michael Leach, then teaching at Penzance School of Art, in 1953. Robin was studying for his Diploma in Art and Design and taking sculpture with Barbara Tribe and design with John Tunnard. Under Michael's tuition he became more interested in ceramics and during weekends and holidays worked at the Leach Pottery helping fire the climbing kiln and throwing and glazing.

At this time Bernard had returned from travelling in the USA and Japan with Hamada and Yanagi, after the Dartington Conference of 1952. 'I particularly remember the chats around the fire place in the workshop during tea breaks, with Bernard expounding on some philosophical subject - which was mostly above my head at the time.' His experience at the Leach Pottery, 'influenced many of the ideas and techniques I have used over my 40 years as a potter.'

In 1965, after a period in Australia, he established Stradbroke Pottery in Suffolk. He never forgot the outback landscape which influences his work and accepted the invitation to return to Australia for a year as craftsman-in-residence during 1979-80. Two years later he completed a residency at Indiana University, USA. He is also a visiting lecturer at many colleges of art and was a member of the 3D Design Board for the Council for National Academic Awards. Among several commissions he made a large pot for the late Dame Elizabeth Frink.

As well as exhibiting his pots widely he created ceramic designs for Wedgwood, Midwinter, Rose of England Bone China and Denby.

Pots, manganese, copper lustre

Vase, stoneware, manganese and copper lustre

Derek Emms

Born: Accrington, Lancs 1929-2004
Studied: Accrington & Burnley Schools of Art and Leeds College
Leach Pottery: 1954-1962
Lived/worked in Stone, Staffordshire, UK

'I'm sure in my own mind that Bernard was not telling people the only way to make pots was like him. He was more concerned with quality, sincerity and a love and feeling for the craft.'

Derek Emms

Derek Emms, inspired by Bernard Leach's *A Potter's Book* studied ceramics at college and also became a qualified teacher but, after completing his National Service in the Royal Air Force, he applied for a job at the Leach Pottery. He worked there under David and Bernard Leach for a very intensive year.

'I still remember vividly my first view of St Ives and Porthminster Beach as the train drew into the station. I came overnight and was met by David Leach at the station. This was 1954 and Bernard was away in America at the time. David was between terms at Loughborough College.' The pottery was led by Michael Leach, with Bill Marshall as foreman, but both Bernard and David returned. The pottery team included Kenneth Quick, Scott Marshall, Dinah Dunn, Horatio Dunn, Richard Batterham, Peter Wood, Joe Benney, and overseas students from Canada, New Zealand and Australia.

In 1955 he became a full-time lecturer at North Staffs Polytechnic but continued his connection by working at the Leach Pottery through summer vacations from 1955-62. He has exhibited his work both at home and abroad throughout his life. He retired from teaching in 1985 and

developed a studio pottery at Stone, in Staffordshire, producing a range of domestic ware and individual pieces in stoneware and porcelain. 'It was at St Ives that I learnt about firing in a reducing atmosphere and this I still do.'

Plant pot 15cm high 21.5cm diameter. Ginger jar 17cm high 15cm diameter

Teapot with cane handle, Tenmoku

All Derek's work is thrown and turned on the wheel using a light coloured stoneware body and a translucent porcelain body. The main skill he developed at the Leach Pottery was throwing, because of the repetitive nature of producing domestic ware, 'but there were so many and varied stimuli that everything must have contributed to my own development.' His decorative techniques included engraving in the leather hard clay, and brush decoration on the biscuit under transparent and translucent glazes.

Many of his patterns evolved from the study of textile design and from flowers, plants and trees, reflecting his life in the countryside.

Len Castle CBE

Born: Auckland, New Zealand 1924
Studied: B.Sc. University of New Zealand
Leach Pottery: 1956-1957
Lives/works in Auckland, N.Z

'I was loaned the only copy in New Zealand of A Potter's Book *by Bernard Leach. The chapter "Towards a Standard" engendered my philosophy about pottery as a means of expression.'*

Len Castle

Len Castle was introduced to pottery at the age of 10 when he watched a demonstration of pottery making, and a childhood discovery of clay at the beach influenced his development as a potter. The 1950s was a decade in which he accumulated and synthesised many influences and developed a personal ceramic language. In 1956 a scholarship took him to Cornwall to study at the Leach Pottery, where he learnt a disciplined work pattern, which enabled him to become a successful potter in his own right. 'I have such pleasant and strongly felt memories of St Ives and life at the Leach Pottery during 1956-57.'

He studied the ceramic collections in England and was especially attracted to the pottery of ancient China, Korea and Japan, and the contemporary examples of Hamada's pots in the same tradition. Later, during Hamada's visit to New Zealand, he watched him demonstrating pots on the wheel, making fast intuitive decisions when the form of the pot was at its vital phase.

An Arts Council Fellowship funded a visit to Japan in 1966, where he was welcomed at the village of Mashiko and rekindled his friendship with Atsuya Hamada, with whom he had worked at the St Ives Pottery. He also visited the Kanjiro Kawai workshop in Kyoto where his pots were fired in a wood-fired multi-chambered climbing kiln. He returned frequently to Japan to study its many potteries.

During the past 32 years Len's workshops and showrooms have been associated with his various homes in Titirangi, where his pots share space with books, paintings, rock samples, fossils, minerals and crystals. His spirituality comes from a close and harmonious relationship with nature.

'Those of us who work with clay can be called alchemists and visual poets. We can set our language, cadences and stanzas in form, colour and texture. As alchemists we can coax magic from seemingly inert clay. We can call on the flame to exert its power and show its fiery palette. We can call on inert materials to undergo transmutations. We can arrange a marriage of passion between intensely heated molecules. Their children will be colour and texture.'

Len was awarded a C.B.E. in the New Year Honour's List in 1986. In recognition of Len Castle's contribution to the world of ceramics, he was granted an Icon Award by the Arts Foundation of New Zealand.

Pouring bottle with looped handle 25.5cm high

Vase, stoneware 31.5cm high

Anne Kjaersgaard

Born: Copenhagen, Denmark 1933-c1980s
Studied: Ecole des Beaux-arts
Leach Pottery: 1956-1958
Lived/worked in France

Bernard Leach said, "You can begin next Monday." 'It was certainly one of Anne's great moments in life. She was so happy.'
Tonna Kjaersgaard

Anne Kjaersgaard

Anne Kjaersgaard regarded herself as a European potter, with roots in Denmark, England and France. She had a know-how of dealing with clay and fire that is from the East and the feeling of her work was oriental, but impregnated by English tradition. After three years at the Arts and Crafts School in Copenhagen she came to the St Ives Pottery and from there to France to study and work from 1958 to 1960 at Saint-Amand en Puisaye; she threw and produced in different workshops, Ateliers Gaulier and Pierre Lyon, amongst others.

She rented a workshop and started to make her own pottery in 1960. Her first firing was like a hatching or an opening of promises and Kjaersgaard the potter was born. She thought that however many metaphors the clay goes through, whether carved, sculpted and monumental, or pulled, flattened, stretched, it is simply 'potting.' Her forms were traditional, jugs, plates, bottles, bowls. She did not depart from their utilitarian destination. 'I am a potter,' was how she defined herself.

'The most important element of her training and the essential of her job as a potter, was working in glazes at the Leach Pottery.' (Elizabeth Gaymard.) She experimented and manipulated natural materials over a long period. The glazes were transparent or deep but always sumptuous. She did not lay down a formula and decorated very quickly, using swift brush strokes in an uninterrupted movement, as if writing. An extremely simplified vocabulary tells of the sea and the waves, the undulations of corn in the wind, the branches of a tree, or a bird.

In 1976 she was invited by the University of Boulder in America, to visit for a term of teaching. During her seven months she built a kiln, to the amazement of the students who were expecting something much less ambitious.

Anne lived near Villeneuve sur Lot in France in 1979. By chance she found a kiln to rent at la Borne. The making of pottery in Europe has always been in the traditional domestic style, of shaping very spontaneously, where all the movements of the hands of the potter remain; the impurities in the clay, marks from turning, finger prints, hand prints that have seized the pot only just finished off the wheel. These things she admired; the way handles were put on and accidents and deformations which occurred in the firing, all added to the decoration.

Vase decorated lustre glaze

Jug with lustre glaze

Peter Stichbury

Born: New Zealand 1924
Studied: Auckland Teachers' Training College
Leach Pottery: 1957
Lives/works in Manurewa, Auckland, New Zealand

'Bernard was an inspiration to many potters in New Zealand. It was an opportunity to work in a team, to increase and hone my pottery skills and become more confident in my own abilities.'

Peter Stichbury

Peter Stichbury, on a Fellowship from the Association of New Zealand Art Societies, and accompanied by his wife Diane, spent seven months at the St Ives Pottery in 1957, followed by nine months in Nigeria, which expanded his horizons considerably. In 1959, back in New Zealand he developed the pottery at Ardmore Teachers' College to its full potential, purchasing ten locally made Leach type wheels and building a kiln. Visiting lecturers to the courses included Bernard Leach, Shoji Hamada, Takeichi Kawai, Michael Cardew and Harry Davis.

In 1963 Peter bought a large old house in three quarters of an acre and established a kiln shed and workshop. By the time he resigned his lectureship at Ardmore College, he was fully prepared to begin potting full time. His pots are domestic ware, a range of casseroles, teapots, coffee sets, oil bottles and everything that can be thrown on the wheel. Glazes are traditional tenmoku and a variety of celadons 'which reflect the lovely soft hues of our New Zealand environment.' Decoration is through wax resist, iron or cobalt with simple brushwork patterns. Diane is a partner in the workshop making a range of moulded dishes which Peter glazes, decorates and fires.

Peter follows Cardew's philosophy which allows a sense of freedom in the art of throwing, and a reinterpretation each time a form is thrown. 'A principle of mine is to make pots to please myself. This is not a conceit, but a necessity if one is to maintain standards and direction, and to develop as a person. In pleasing myself, hopefully I will also please others.' He prefers to use natural materials and for many years dug and processed a local stoneware clay. He developed a body clay from commercial products with additions of feldspar and ochre.

Teapot, barium glaze over Tenmoku 16.5cm high

He particularly enjoys making large platters. An iron sand pattern is freely applied while the glaze is still wet, which requires speed and skill. One of these platters was selected as a gift to Queen Elizabeth from the New Zealand Government.

In 2002 Peter was awarded Member of the New Zealand Order of Merit for services to Pottery.

Screw stopper bottle, stoneware

Richard Batterham

Born: 1936
Studied: Bryanston Public School
Leach Pottery: 1957-1958
Lives/works in Blandford, Dorset, UK

'Batterham has always known where he was going and by the time he left St Ives he had planned his future in some detail.' Muriel Rose

Richard Batterham

Richard Batterham showed an interest in pottery from an early age and was fortunate to attend Bryanston school where boys were encouraged to learn about the craft. The school workshop was run by Donald Potter who gave the pupils time to practise their skills on the wheel and learn how to master the wood-fired kiln. This early learning was a distinct advantage when he applied to work at the Leach pottery.

During his year of study at the Leach Pottery, he was fortunate to meet Atsuya Hamada, the son of Shoji, who was on a visit from Japan and was furthering his studies at St Ives. Working on the permanent staff of the pottery was Dinah Dunn, who trained at the Hull College of Art, Yorkshire, and developed into a fine potter in her own right. She spent about five years at the St Ives pottery, mastering all the techniques. She later married Richard, giving up her own interest in ceramics to look after their large family of children.

Working at the pottery helped further Richard's ambition to be a potter in his own right and after leaving St Ives, he and his wife bought a cottage in Durweston, near Blandford in Dorset. He built an oil-fired two-chambered climbing kiln and began potting straight away. He produced well designed stoneware of a domestic type on a small scale until, after six years, he completed the building for a larger workshop close to home and was able to extend his range of pots.

Richard Batterham is regarded by some as one of the finest makers of domestic stoneware in the Leach tradition. Although he remains true to his intention of making pots that 'enrich rather than adorn life,' he has further extended his range and produced pots that are not just strictly useful. The designs are semi-matt celadons with minimal decoration. He works entirely alone at his craft, firing the kiln five or six times a year.

Standard size teapot, stoneware 15cm high

The design is based on a Japanese climbing kiln similar to that at the Leach Pottery.

'As in all the making and firing, preconceptions must be forgotten, and an open mind kept, able to receive the good unknown qualities which will appear. One must not dictate, but listen, observe and respond.' [24]

Bottle vase, stoneware, 34cm high

Atsuya Hamada

Born: Mashiko, Japan 1931-1986
Studied: Mooka High School
Leach Pottery: 1957-1958
Lived/worked in Mashiko, Japan

'He faithfully used the method he learned at the Leach Pottery on how to make handles.'

Atsuya Hamada

Atsuya Hamada was very much influenced in style by Bernard and David Leach. He was the third son of Shoji Hamada and also trained with him. In 1972 he had his first solo exhibition at Mitsukoshi Nihonbashi department store in Tokyo, and every year after that. He died in Mashiko at the early age of 54 years and was at that time trying to steer away from the very strong influences of his training to find his own method and style. He knew Bernard Leach from the visits he made to his father at Mashiko. He wanted to be a potter and to study at the Leach Pottery. In 1949 he wrote to Bernard.

'We received your letter at the beginning of December. It was the second one we had from Europe after the war. We received your first letter in December 1947, and we wrote you a letter with our news and some photos, but are afraid it did not arrive.'

'I wonder if you remember Mashiko when I was quite young. I am now nineteen years old. At present seven potters are working with my father. Firing of the big kiln was just done yesterday and unloading will be on the fifth of January. Many big houses were built (big studio, big house larger than the former house, big kiln which has eight chambers, another gate-

house, and so on). You will be surprised to see them. I can make many pots (vases, cups, tea-pots, dishes, bowls, and so on). I will become a potter. I wish to go to St Ives some day to learn European techniques, and am anxious to know if you will kindly teach me.' [28]

Atsuya achieved his ambition to work with Bernard and in 1957 arrived at the St Ives Pottery.

He was well-liked by the pottery crew. He brought a fresh oriental approach to the standard-ware and new pottery techniques in the use of bamboo and wood tools. His ascetic sensibility showed in his throwing and turning. He was a great friend of Bill Marshall and shared his interest in botany and geology. He was fond of wild flowers, especially the anemones, which grew in the surrounding hills. He dug up some of these to send to his mother in Japan.

Left: *Lidded water container*

Right: *Pitcher, brushed colour overglazes*

Helena Klug

Born: Recife, Brazil
Studied: Chateau de Ratilly, France
Leach Pottery: 1958
Lives/Works Paris, France

'These three months were very rich and I often had the opportunity to talk with him and it is there that my passion for glazes was born.'

Helena Klug

Helena Klug nee da Silva first heard about Bernard Leach in 1957 at Ratilly and this made her want to meet him. Her English was virtually non-existent, but she found someone willing to write to Bernard on her behalf. In 1958, although she had had no answer to her letter, she took the risk and visited St Ives.

Bernard Leach welcomed her and admitted that he had not replied to the letter because he had not taken to the handwriting. However, at the end of the interview he was willing to give her a placement for a month; an exceptional privilege, the rule being that students were taken on for two years. In the end Helena stayed for three months, by which time she had to return to Brazil.

At the Leach pottery at that time were, Anne Kjaersgaard, Atsuya Hamada, Dinah and Richard Batterham. Each was responsible for a part of the current production from throwing to glazing. 'It was William Marshall, who was in charge of the workshop and explained to me what I had to do. Leach's personal studio was set apart but you very much felt his presence. He came through the workshop every day and would often make observations.'

Bowl, decorated 25cm diameter

With Helena's imminent departure for Brazil she asked Bernard many questions. He would sometimes gather the students together to talk about clays, glazes and shapes. 'A lot of what he told us appears in *A Potter's Book* but I still have my notes written down at the time.' After a discussion about glazes he made them do tests with ashes, clays, feldspar, ball-clay, kaolin, silica, talc, and then commented on the results.

'I did not see him until twenty years later. A year before his death I was able to revisit St Ives with my husband. Leach living alone, his flat facing the sea, invited us to dinner. He talked a lot to us about the East and the West and with such presence that it was difficult to realise that he had become blind.'

Helena is best known for her courses in stoneware and for her own rigorous and genuine pottery, infused with harmony. It features rich colours, simple designs with brush wax resist or dipping of colour over glazes. She enlivens her vases, plates and bowls with a range of hues of reds, kaki, blue and some creamy whites, at times tinged by celadon greens. She aims to make domestic pottery beautiful by its functionality.

Plate, decorated 30cm diameter

Gwyn Hanssen Pigott

Born: Ballarat, Australia 1935
Studied: University of Melbourne, Australia
Leach Pottery: 1958-1959
Lives/works in Queensland, Australia

'Leach's personal philosophy and charisma was strong, and I was introduced to wares I had seldom touched or examined before, Chinese, Korean and Japanese.'

Gwyn Hanssen Pigott

Gwyn Hanssen Pigott bicycled down to St Ives from London shortly after arriving in Britain in 1958. She met Bernard at the Leach Pottery and gave him, as a gift from Ivan McMeekin, a blue celadon-glazed porcelain dish which Ivan had made. She had been apprenticed to McMeekin in Australia and was due to work with Michael Cardew, during his leave from Africa, at Wenford Bridge. She worked also for Ray Finch at Winchcombe Pottery. At St Ives her contacts with Janet Leach, John Reeve, Pierre Culot, Michael Henry, Clary Illian and other 'fellow pilgrims,' were all inspirational.

In 1960 she organised her first workshop with Louis Hanssen in Westbourne Grove, London. They got to know Lucie Rie, a walk away, and through her Hans Coper - 'Both pivotal for us.' Gwyn also worked at Alan Caiger-Smith's London workshop, having first met him at Cardew's, along with Henry Hammond, Paul Barron and Helen Pincombe. From 1966 to 1973 she was in France renting a workshop and firing in Anne Kjaersgaard's kiln and then establishing a pottery at Acheres, near Bourges. On returning to Australia in 1973 she set up workshops in Tasmania, and currently has her studio near Brisbane, South East

Queensland, where she works alone.

Her present pots are translucent porcelain, gas and wood-fired. She makes 'seemingly' simple bottles, beakers, jugs, cups, and bowls and other flared or straight shapes in 'still life' groups, or 'parades.' 'The still life groups have evolved gradually, out of the dual pleasures of using and looking. There are obvious influences from painters, Morandi is one; perhaps Ben Nicholson another and my visits to Brancusi's studio in Paris in my early twenties.'

Her groups of pots play on the changes of surface and luminosity as much as on colour, form and line. She is intrigued by the fine line between the monotonous and the lively, the dull and the subtle.

'In almost forty years historical and personal influences are distilled. There has been China, Asia, Britain and Europe - but the work seems to follow itself. There are constants: the scale is domestic, the matter vitrified, the pots functional. Hopefully they invite quiet contemplation and handling.'

Above: *Still life with teapot & cup, porcelain*

Below: *Still life with bowl, porcelain*

John Reeve

Born: Vancouver, British Columbia, Canada 1929
Studied: Travelled extensively
Leach Pottery: 1958-1961 & 1966
Lives/works in Canada

'John was gentle, modest, lovable; there was a soul behind his searching eyes.' Bernard Leach

John Reeve

John Reeve was known to Bernard before he came to work at the Leach Pottery. Bernard had flown to Canada in the early 1950s for a series of workshops and was met at Seattle airport by John and his wife Donna. Bernard recalls, 'We talked and talked for hours, knitting up the ravelled sleeve of time and care. I think it was the next day we parted, almost in tears.' Bernard invited John to come and work with him at the Leach Pottery. He arrived with his wife Donna in 1958 and while in St Ives Donna gave birth to their first child.

It was Bernard who introduced John to Warren Mackenzie and his wife Alix, the first two American potters who came to work at the Leach Pottery. Thereafter they became friends and worked together for some months at St Paul and Minneapolis. Both Warren Mackenzie and John Reeve kept in touch with Bernard over many years by talking on tape and circulating the cassettes.

Other companions at the Leach Pottery were Glenn Lewis, a fellow Canadian, Byron Temple, American, Gwyn Hanssen-Pigott, Australian, Pierre Culot, Belgium, Kenneth Quick, Richard Batterham and his wife Dinah Dunn, and John Leach, Bernard's grandson. William Marshall was foreman, and Janet Leach had not long married Bernard and taken charge of the pottery. It was quite a mixture of personalities and backgrounds. While in Cornwall John received a grant from the Canadian Council to build a pottery in Hennock, Devon.

In 1966, on the invitation of Janet Leach, who described John as, 'a very good potter,' he returned to the pottery, but this second visit was not a success. It was not a happy experience for John, 'I find some things too painful to remember.' And yet the friendship survived. Bernard said of him in his memoirs *Beyond East and West* '..his lovable nature and ingenuity always brought forgiveness in its wake.' During this visit to St Ives John was fortunate to meet Shoji Hamada and his wife. He also spent some time teaching pottery at Farnham College of Art.

On his return to Canada John Reeve became a well-known name in pottery.

Yellow pot, porcelain

Bowl, stoneware with ash glaze

Mansimran Singh

Born: Lahore, India, 1939
Studied: Delhi. Senior Cambridge Exam.
Leach Pottery: 1959-60
Lives/works: Andretta Pottery, Kangra, India

'As a teacher I am confident that Leach's stringent teaching methods have helped me to impart high standards and values to my students.'

Mansimran Singh

Mansimran Singh first learnt about basic packing techniques when he began his time at the pottery. Leach's attitude to packing was that until you know how to get the pot to the buyer, you shouldn't think of making a pot. And then came a good and rigorous grounding in throwing. After this he had to make interminable numbers of egg bakers until Bernard approved their exact nature.

Leach was a devotee of the Baha'i faith and he and Singh had many interesting discussions about religion. 'Bernard sometimes called us to his house for talks about pottery in a rather formal atmosphere – encouraging us to criticise certain pots – giving our impressions and views. In the work place he was a very hard taskmaster and a great disciplinarian.' This had a good effect on the standards Singh set for his own work, remembering how all sub-standard pottery was scrupulously broken. There used to be "seconds" at the Leach Pottery but never a second by Bernard Leach.

During his time in St Ives he worked with the potters, William Marshall, Scott Marshall, John Reeve from Canada, Richard Jenkins, Janet Leach and Horatio Dunn, the packer. Johnny Leach came later and for a while they were contemporaries.

Like his father, also a potter, Mansimran has tended towards utilitarian pottery, as well as classical shapes. This was mainly due to the Japanese influence on both Leach and his father. He never visited Japan, and after returning to India from England, his pottery took on something from the Indian tradition in shape and design.

Two years ago he visited the Leach Pottery and found it to be much the same and it invoked a lot of memories. He was pleased to find a potter still working there and selling her pots. Now he is working and teaching far away at the foot of the Himalayas, using local earthenware clay. The Andretta Pottery specialises in earthenware with slipped geometrical designs reminiscent of the patterns made on the floor by Indian women for their prayer ceremonies.

Stoneware bottle, furglaze 32cm high

Stoneware bottle, tenmoku glaze 30cm high

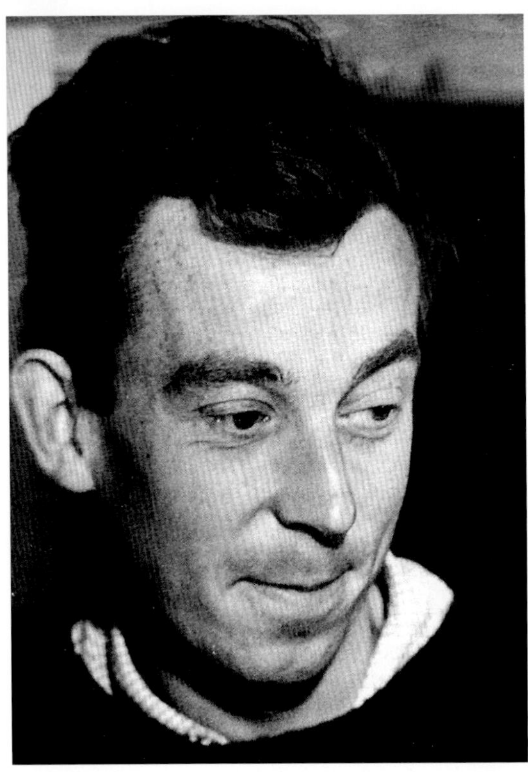

Richard Jenkins

Born: Maidstone, Kent 1932-1965
Studied: Arts and Crafts, Maidstone College of Art
Leach Pottery: 1959-1961

'Richard came to the Leach Pottery because he wanted to experience the daily making of pots and to benefit from Bernard's teaching.'

Richard Jenkins

Richard Jenkins prepared himself over a number of years for his goal of being accepted for work experience at the Leach Pottery and absorbing the benefits of an intense potter's environment by studying Arts and Crafts at his Maidstone College. He went on to specialise in ceramics and gained a National Diploma in Design at Stoke-on-Trent College of Art. He then worked as a ceramic designer at Johnson Mathay in London. In 1958 he completed his Art Teacher's Diploma at Goldsmiths College, London, where he gained a distinction.

One year later, with these qualifications, Richard set out to gain entry to the Leach Pottery and was successful. The daily making of pots, handling clay, experimenting with glazes, firing the kiln being part of the crew and engaged fully in the experience of being a work-a-day potter completed his intense training.

Richard gained benefit from working with a team of dedicated potters, all proficient in many fields of pottery but, like himself, wishing to partake in the daily task of honing their skills in the sheer hard work of producing the standard ware to the precise requirements of the Leach Pottery production line, and to Bernard's critical and exacting standards. During

Jug and mugs, ash glaze

his time at the Leach Pottery his colleagues were, Bill Marshall, Kenneth Quick, Pamela Greenwood, John Leach, Atsuya Hamada from Japan, and others from around the world all anxious to work at the pottery.

After three years at the Leach Pottery he was awarded the first scholarship, offered by the Japanese Government, to work in Japan studying pottery and ceramics. After considerable soul-searching, he decided to stay in Cornwall and start his own pottery.

In 1961 Richard asked Scott Marshall if he would consider coming into partnership in a pottery at Boscean, St Just, Cornwall. Together they converted and built the workshop and showroom and the then largest, Japanese style, climbing kiln in the country. They produced well-designed porcelain and stoneware oven and tableware, using clays and glazes that reflected the colours and ambience of West Cornwall. The large kiln enabled them to make pots at a prolific rate.

Pot, wood ash glaze 16cm high. Pot, wood ash glaze 8.5cm high

Richard, apart from being a sensitive and expert craftsman, was also a good business man. He contacted galleries and shops throughout Britain which stocked their products. Alongside this Richard made individual pots using techniques, shapes, and glazes that captured his own deepest feelings. Many of these are in collections in this country and abroad. Richard and Scott also held exhibitions of their individual work in various venues, including The Craftsman Potters Shop in London.

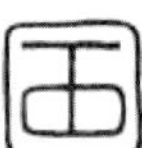

Byron Temple

Born: Centerville, Indiana, USA 1933
Studied: Ball State University, Brooklyn Museum School, Art Institute of Chicago
Leach Pottery: 1959-1961
Lives/works in Louisville, Kentucky, USA

'Part of my early training in St Ives involved making things simply and quickly, and in volume, to get them out for a price the public could afford.'

Byron Temple

Byron Temple doesn't like pots that are derivative. He makes his own pots with sleek, slim, simple lines and vigorous throwing, with marks left exposed - not trying to cover anything up. 'That's me, my mentality, what I call my ceramic intellect.'

He enjoys creating tableware and is proud to be seen in the tradition of domestic ware potters. He has championed the cause of functional pots throughout his career. As well as making a living he imbues his pots with aesthetic and spiritual value, although he does not attempt to sell his pots as art.

The strong influence of his years of working with Bernard Leach enabled Byron to produce tableware which is straight-forward, restrained and inviting. He has been described as a 'clay guru' by some of his students, but he prefers to be seen simply as a teacher. When he studied with Leach he went there 'to learn not to worship,' or to make heroes. He sometimes found the atmosphere too precious and was not without critical comment, especially when, in 1978 he returned to the Leach Pottery as manager, after Bill Marshall left. Both Bernard and Janet approved the appointment because of Byron's experience in training his own team and his successful business, but he returned to the States to continue running his own personal pottery.

From 1962 to 1989 Byron successfully operated his pottery/workshop in Lambertville, New Jersey, where he produced 'a range of wood-fired table-ware and individual saggar-fired pots with a dark, intense coloured body.'

On a tour of New Zealand, organised by the New Zealand Society of Potters, Byron's honesty and straight forwardness endeared him to potters who attended his workshops and demonstrations. He also travelled to the European Ceramics Work Centre in the Netherlands and was one of only 17 from 120 applicants from 23 countries to be accepted for a residency .He exhibited his work at Museum Boymans-van Beuningen, in Rotterdam in 1995 and at a mixed show at Galerie Besson, London.

Visitors to an exhibition at the State Museum New Jersey, where he showed 61 examples of stoneware and porcelain domestic ware, were encouraged to handle his work. Byron now lives and works quietly in Louisville, Kentucky. 'I've danced on the tables, now I want to give my pots more thought.'

Left: *Tea jar, porcelain saggar fired 13cm high*

Right: *Tie box 14cm high*

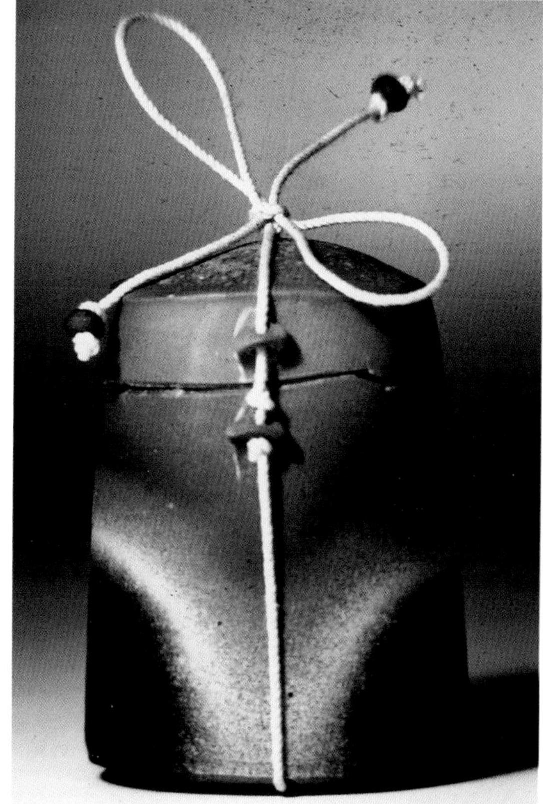

John Leach

Born: Pottery Cottage, St Ives, Cornwall 1939
Studied: with David Leach, Ray Finch, Colin Pearson
Leach Pottery: 1960-1963
Lives/works at Muchelney Pottery, Somerset, UK

'He would talk about pots in relation to other arts, music or poetry. He would tell me to look at a 13th century jug and then I knew and understood what he had described in words.'

John Leach

John Leach is happy as a third generation potter in the Leach line. He was taught to make pots that have integrity, that one feels sincere about. 'Making shapes that I have designed, that are blessed with fire, that people buy to give you a living - to be able to do that is wonderful. I feel privileged that society has allowed me to live in this way.'

Before returning to St Ives John worked with his father David, Ray Finch, and Colin Pearson. 'It humbled me to work with grandfather. At the age of 20 I thought I could show what throwing was about.' After working all week making standard ware from the catalogue the students were encouraged to produce work of their own choosing. 'My pots came out of the kiln and were put beside the others to await criticism. Grandfather paused before mine and said, "Too much up here, (pointing to his head) not enough here, (pointing to his stomach) and your tail is wagging."'

When he left the Leach Pottery in 1963 he helped set up a pottery with Harold Guilland in California and taught at summer school. Through the years he has continued to study pots from different centuries and cultures. He travelled to Nigeria to observe the large bellied coiled pots made by women potters, and likes the early American stoneware whiskey jugs, as well as admiring the work of many contemporary potters. 'When I drink a cup of coffee I choose a mug made by one of my many potter friends. In that way I can commune with that person.'

John's stoneware is robust, serviceable and traditional. He enjoys making bowls, and all turned ware. He uses West Country clays. 'I love wood firing. The best pots at St Ives came from the second chamber, which was wood-fired. I love that unpredictable, toasted effect from the fly ash.' The wood burned is from used timber. He has planted trees in several acres he bought from a local farmer and is replacing this renewable resource, returning to nature that which helped him to create in clay.

Muchelney Pottery, a thatched cottage in Somerset, is a wonderful working and living environment where he makes pots for eating, drinking and enjoying.

Facetted bottle, wood-fired stoneware with ash glaze on khaki 23cm high

Dish, sawdust fired in saggar 21.5cm diameter

Nirmala Patwardhan

Born: Hyderabad, Pakistan 1928
Studied: Art at Santiniketan
Leach Pottery: 1961
Lives/works at home in India

'Bernard would sometimes cook Cornish pasty and I would make Indian curries. Can you believe that it was Bernard who taught me how to cook rice! Bernard was a wonderful person.'

Nirmala Patwardhan

Nirmala Patwardhan's initiation into pottery was in Stuttgart, Germany, under Professor Ulrich Gunther at the State Academy of Stuttgart in 1958. The emphasis under the Professor was more on glazes than on throwing.

On her return to India she started working and held an exhibition of her work in 1961. She was not satisfied with her own work in spite of critical acclaim, so later that year she landed in England to learn about pottery. It was Lucie Rie, who she had met earlier, who advised her to contact Ray Finch at Winchcombe Pottery. 'I worked under him as an apprentice for one month. Thereafter, at Ray's suggestion, I went to Farnham and studied under Henry Hammond. A few weeks later I got a letter from Janet Leach to come to the Leach Pottery.'

After three months in Farnham Nirmala came to the St Ives Pottery and began her apprenticeship with Bernard Leach. This was the result of a recommendation by Lucie Rie. It was a wonderful experience and she got her first real practice of potting. Almost every evening, Bernard would visit Glen Lewis, a Canadian student, and Nirmala and talk about Japan, his experience with Raku and how he became a potter.

Bowl, chun blue glaze, reduction fired, feldspar, ash and flint 20.5cm dia

Pot, Tenmoku, made at Leach Pottery 1962

After the regular work was over they were free to stay on at the pottery to make their own pots and experiment with glazes. Bernard would come and critically comment on their work. Nirmala had learned a fair amount about glazes in Germany so could experiment on her own.

'My son, who was quite young visited me at St Ives. He could only come to the pottery after five o'clock, but most of the time I was still working on my pots. Bernard would take out his chess board and both of them would be playing until I became free.'

All the workers at the Leach Pottery were extremely friendly and kind. They admired her ability to make different glazes. 'I understand from William Marshall, who was the pottery foreman during my time, that there is still a bucketful of Nirmala Patwardhan Tenmoku glaze at the pottery, which he used regularly. After I left it was called the N Glaze.' In 2005 Nirmala enlarged and published a new edition of her book *New Handbook for Potters*, written mainly for Indian potters and students.

Glenn Lewis

Born: Chemainus, B.C. 1935
Studied: Painting, drawing, ceramics, Vancouver School of Art
Leach Pottery: 1961-1963
Lives/works: Roberts Creek B.C.

'What I learned from Leach, other potters and the making of pots was that there was great meaning in the most ordinary things and in the process in making them.'

Glenn Lewis

Glenn Lewis after graduating in painting and ceramics from art school and teacher training at the University of B.C. Vancouver, decided to write to Bernard Leach. This was on the advice of his friend, John Reeve, who had worked at the famous St Ives pottery in 1958. When he arrived he was put to work by William Marshall. He worked alongside Kenneth Quick, John Leach, Patricia Ashmore and Nirmala Patwarden. As an apprentice he worked from 8 to 5 every weekday making useful and ordinary standard ware. 'You start with hors' d'oeurve dishes (often used as ash trays) and egg bakers. You repeat these set-shaped pieces until your efforts are good enough to keep.'

This process can take from two weeks to two months, or more. 'Your speed of throwing increases – this is mainly due to limiting unnecessary movements – taking two pulls instead of three and not going back over it.' This initial mastery of forms and materials was only the first step. Later, when Glenn had made the necessary strides to perfect throwing and gained his experience of making pots, he turned to making sculptural pieces. Because of that necessary, strict, repetitive routine, he approached the more difficult phases of progress as an ordinary part of his life.

After his apprenticeship in 1963 he teamed up with John Reeve to build the pottery at Longlands, Hennock in Devon. In 1964 he returned to Vancouver to teach ceramics and sculpture at the University of British Columbia. 'From that point on I produced sculpture, correspondence art, prints, photo-based works, and performances, singly and collaboratively, with several communities of artists.'

Making ordinary pottery had given Glenn a viewpoint on creating and inspiration, 'a microcosm that I could look out from and understand how everything else worked and how to proceed to work with everything and everyone.'

In 2004 an exhibition of ceramic works took place at the Morris and Helen Belkin Art Gallery of the University of British Columbia. Showing were 800 pieces under the title "Thrown," celebrating the Vancouver studio pottery movement of 1960s and 1970s. The movement was in part, influenced by the British studio pottery advocate, Bernard Leach. It was based on the influence of Leach and Japanese sensibilities and featured the work of John Reeve, Michael Henry, Glenn Lewis, Ian Steele, William Marshall, Kenneth quick, Bernard and Janet Leach and Shoji Hamada, who were among those potters who shared the Leach legacy. Other potters were also included and a catalogue printed to celebrate the event.

Lidded stoneware pot and vase

Two lugged vases and a mug

Shinsaku Hamada

Born: Tokyo 1929
Studied: Arts and Crafts, Waseda University
Leach Pottery: 1963
Lives/works in Mashiko, Japan

'Shinsaku Hamada is 21. He is making pots and will become a potter.' A letter from Atsuya Hamada to Bernard Leach 1949

Shinsaku Hamada

Shinsaku Hamada was the second son of Shoji Hamada. He was born in Tokyo but moved with his family to Mashiko in 1930. In 1950 he studied arts and crafts and industrial arts and technology at Waseda University. After University he began an apprenticeship with his father at the pottery in Mashiko

In 1963 Shinsaku visited St Ives with Hamada to renew their friendship with Bernard and Janet Leach. They travelled together for a year in America where Hamada was lecturing and demonstrating and also visited Mexico, Europe and the Middle East. It was a great experience for the young Shinsaku, who acted as assistant to his father.

In 1970 Shinsaku had his first solo exhibition at Mitsukoshi Nihonbashi department store, in Tokyo. In 1976/77 he had solo exhibitions all over Japan and became a member of the National Artists Association (Kokugakai). He was also appointed director of the Mashiko Reference Collection Museum, for which Shoji Hamada was largely responsible for collecting furniture and artifacts in arts and crafts, many from England.

To widen his experience of ceramics Shinsaku visited the kilns in Korea, China and Taiwan. In 1985 he took part in a three-man exhibition of ceramics at Liberty Department Store in London with Kenji Funaki from Matsue and Tatsuzo Shimaoka, with whom he works at Mashiko. He celebrated forty years as a potter in 1989 and held his twentieth one-man exhibition at Mitsukoshi Store, Nihonbashi, Tokyo.

Seiji Oshima, Director of the Setagaya Art Museum, in writing a foreword for a beautiful book of Shinsaku's works, stated that although he was always under Hamada's wing, 'He himself most seriously recognises that distinction between father and son is imperative. So Shinsaku consciously made an effort to resist and oppose likeness to develop originality.'

Mallet vase, faceted, two ears, black iron glaze

Jar, brushed slip, iron glaze pattern

Mirek Smisek

Born: Bohemia, Czechoslovakia 1925
Studied: Kyoto University, Japan
Leach Pottery: 1963-1964
Lives/works in Aotearoa, New Zealand

'Bernard Leach and I met in Japan in 1962 while I was studying ceramics at the Faculty of Industrial Arts in Kyoto. He invited me to come to St Ives.'

Mirek Smisek

Mirek Smisek came to St Ives to study and work with Bernard Leach in 1963. It was an experience which had the most profound influence on his own work. He was living in New Zealand at the time and the Arts Council of that country helped to finance the trip. He was accompanied by his family. 'It was our great privilege to have Barbara Hepworth, as our landlady. She gave me many opportunities to talk with her about art, which has strengthened my belief in creativity and its vital role for humanity.'

He started potting in 1948. His first workshop was established in Nelson, South Island, New Zealand in 1953. Salt-glazed stoneware was his first venture. For the last quarter of a century his studio-workshop has been in North Island, Te Horo, where he works with his wife and partner, Pamella Ann. They make domestic and decorative stoneware and porcelain and have exhibited widely. As well as developing their own work they encourage children from local schools to be creatively involved and gain practical experience.

Mirek says his aim is to make handmade things with the qualities of natural materials, to set against the machine-made. He makes domestic pots because he believes an article should be made to live with, not to be

Branch pot, fluted

Two jugs

bought and admired on rare occasions. He makes humble shapes, born from the heart and pleasing to the eye, and made as if to use them himself. He compares his approach to the craft with the Japanese tea ceremony. At the centre everything revolves around the humble pot.

'As a potter, my aim is to utilise and highlight the rich textures contained in our clays and rocks. It is important to aim to make a pot which will fulfil our desire and need to surround ourselves with aesthetically healthy objects which should not only be admired for their beauty, but give fulfilment in frequent handling. Pottery, with the exciting challenge of mastery over the elements earth, water and fire, offers tremendous scope for fulfilment. Good results do not come easily, but there is a great adventure for anybody willing to be sincerely involved.'

Michael Henry

Born: New Westminster, British Columbia, Canada 1939
Studied: Graphics and Design Vancouver School of Art, Canada
Leach Pottery: 1963-1965
Lives/works in British Columbia, Canada

"The Leach Pottery was a great influence in my life and I made pots for 15 years with a passion.'

Michael Henry

Michael Henry, after completing his studies at the Vancouver School of Art, concentrated on landscape painting. After a few years he decided to come to England in 1963. He visited St Ives to see Glen Lewis, a fellow Canadian then working at the Leach Pottery. He joined him for a few months, to earn a little money, working as a clay mixer, became interested in the whole process of making pots and the 'communal work sensibility' and applied to work as an apprentice.

Janet took him on and he served an apprenticeship for just over two years. 'Janet Leach was very kind to me as a growing-up potter.' Also there at this time was Mirek Smisek, a potter from New Zealand. Having gained the necessary skills Michael returned to Vancouver and started his own studio, producing glazed stoneware. Two years later he moved to the country about 30 miles North West of Vancouver and built a pottery, making salt-glazed stoneware for the kitchen and table for the local community. This lasted about seven years, when back problems forced him to give up potting.

Since then he has worked in carpentry and house design, and for five years worked in graphics for the Medicine Department at the University

Dish

of Vancouver. After travelling in Europe he returned to his country place where his old 'Slug Pottery' building has become the Slug Meditation Centre, thereby affirming an abiding interest, from his Leach Pottery days, in community life. There he cultivates a large sustainable garden for visitors who come to camp out, and engages in his favourite past time of reading in a serene environment.

An interest in natural materials which was developed at the Leach Pottery, a close intimacy with clay, and the idea of 'back to basics', all atune happily with the simplicity of country living in close harmony with nature.

In 1988 he returned to England, made a trip to Cornwall, visited various friends and Janet Leach at the pottery, and renewed his acquaintance with the small fishing town of St Ives which fostered his love of ceramics.

Jar with lid

Jack Worseldine

Born: Osage, Iowa, USA 1937
Studied: Kansas City Art Institute & School of Design
Leach Pottery: 1963-1965
Lives/works in Sedona, Arizona, USA

'My experience at the Leach Pottery and the day to day contact with Bernard will remain for me an unforgettable experience.'

Jack Worseldine

Jack Worseldine, before engaging in further study and following a career in the arts, served from 1955 to 1959 in the United States Navy. He came to St Ives after completing his degree in fine art. He was a friend of Warren MacKenzie, who had studied with Leach, and helped secure his position at the pottery in August 1963. During his stay in Cornwall he exhibited in St Ives and in the 'Bernard Leach Potters' Exhibition' of 1964 at the British Crafts Centre, London.

He enjoyed a working relationship with Janet Leach during his two years at St Ives and became a close friend of Bill Marshall, whom he considered was a 'great thrower'. He met Shoji Hamada and his son Shinsaku when they visited Janet and Bernard at St Ives, 'which was a privilege for all of us there at the time.' They had travelled from Japan to attend a major exhibition of Hamada's pots at the Haymarket in London in 1963.

On his return to the States Jack studied at the University of Minnesota taking ceramics, graphics and art history and gained his Masters Degree. He taught ceramics, sculpture and life drawing at several schools, colleges, and Arizona State University, whilst also engaged in producing his own pottery. He exhibited in many mixed and solo shows throughout the United States winning two awards for sculpture and ceramics.

His own approach to pottery has always been functional. He enjoys making useful vessels for the kitchen, a variety of tableware, domestic items and garden planters. Although he is still surrounded by many of his pots, he was forced to close his last pottery in 1985 because of an injury to his back and a slipped disc. He now owns and runs an art shop with his wife Mary. Over the period of working with ceramics and teaching, he became a serving member of the American Craftsmen's Council, the Association of University Professors, and the World Crafts Council.

Group of teapots

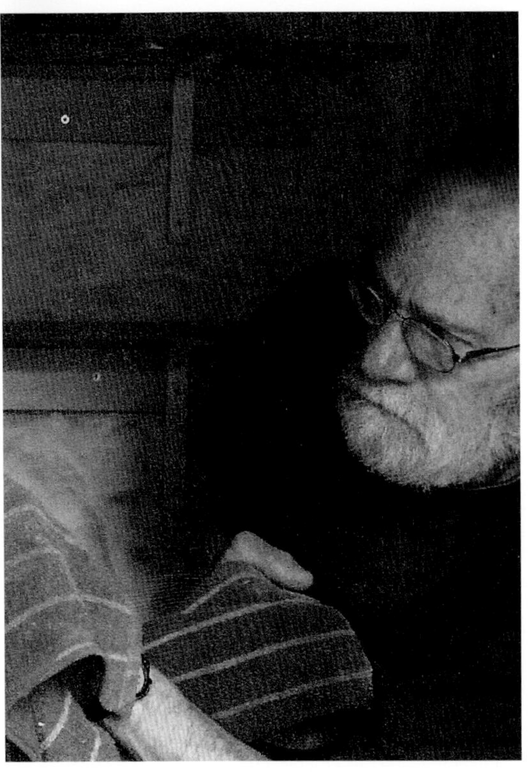

IS

Ian Steele

Born: Saskatchewan, Canada 1937
Studied: Design and Pottery at Vancouver School of Art
Leach Pottery: 1963-1965 & 1967-1969
Lives/works in Chudleigh, Devon, UK

'Those four years have affected my thought process and actions; the way I see things and do things,over the last 30 years.'

Ian Steele

Ian Steele set up his own pottery at Nanoose Bay in British Columbia, Canada, after leaving the Leach Pottery in 1969. For the first four years he specialised in salt glaze pottery but then built another kiln to produce a range of domestic stoneware pottery. Although he returned to England in 1977, Ian's pottery was displayed in 'Thrown' a large exhibition held in 2004 at the University of British Columbia, which charted the influences on West Coast Ceramics, with the Leach Pottery being foremost.

'Perhaps the Leach influence has been so world wide because of the range of students working at the pottery, coming from different countries, with varied backgrounds and experiences and returning home to set up their own studios.'

Ian remembers the exciting experience of Hamada and Shinsaku visiting from Japan in 1963 and watching their expertise in making pots. 'Producing pottery to a high standard was paramount at the Leach Pottery.'

When Ian returned to England he set up his pottery in Chudleigh, Devon, making a range of domestic stoneware pottery influenced by the Leach tradition. Basically, he uses oatmeal, celadons, ash glaze and tenmoku. Ian likes the quality of the celadons, especially over a porcelain base. 'I like the idea of the contrast between the stoneware and the porcelain. There is a total difference between the two, one very earthy, one very delicate and smooth.'

In Chudleigh Ian concentrated on establishing his studio and outlet under one roof, dealing directly with the general public, producing both functional pots as well as exhibition pieces. Within this practice he often experimented with different shapes, clays and glazes, 'the pots are not static for me.' However, in the mid 1990s Ian had converted his workshop and barn into a house and for a few years was unable to produce any pottery. In 2004 he again established his studio on a smaller scale to produce both stoneware and porcelain to exhibit in outlets and galleries.

Pot, salt glaze

'In the end I just feel that I have done what I wanted, in the way I wanted, more or less when I wanted, and was very fortunate. It was an exciting time at the Leach Pottery. Had it not been I would not remember it with such fondness.'

Lugged vase,
oatmeal glaze
9.5cm high

Clary Illian

Born: Iowa, USA 1940
Studied: University of Iowa, USA
Leach Pottery: 1964-1965
Lives/works in Iowa, USA

'Like Bernard I developed a love of articulating what it is that makes a good pot good. When I teach I simply put into words all the things I learnt about form at the Leach Pottery'

Clary Illian

Clary Illian has the fondest memories of her time at the Leach Pottery and immense gratitude for the wonder at finding herself an apprentice. Exposure to the great pottery of Asia and Europe was an 'eye-opener' and helped form her pottery vocabulary. Those pots were more of an influence on her than Bernard's personal work - she thinks that is how he meant it to be - but she cherishes her memories of him and his passion for pots. 'I remember how accessible he was and how easy to ask him to critique my own personally produced ware.'

Although she makes objects for everyday use her notion about the significance of form comes from modernism. Her influences were the sculptors Henry Moore, Jean Arp and Constantin Brancusi as well as the ceramics of Asia and Europe. She built up the anatomy of form in making standard ware, learning to throw pots identical in size and shape as required for the Leach Catalogue. 'I am quite annoyed when I, or someone, is accused of only being a Leach potter because I believe that a Leach potter is influenced by the great pottery of the world.'

She lives and works in a converted Oddfellows Hall. She mixes her clay and glazes from scratch and does high fire reduction glazed firing and has recently built a second kiln. She still uses a Leach wheel and credits it with many of the passions in her work - her preoccupation with gesture as it interacts with silhouette.

She works in both stoneware and porcelain, selling a range of domestic ware of quality. 'I do not produce a standard ware but if I have arrived at a shape which I think works well and holds some interest for me I will repeat. Fortunately my customers come right along with me when I do something new.' She identifies herself as a crafts person who produces work of the highest quality. Clary is not a decorator. The involvement with wheel-thrown forms makes her trust that the pots will be of lasting value for the user, in terms of utility and their provocative or meditative content.

White jug

White vase

TC:

Trevor Corser

Born: Oldham 1938
Studied: Apprentice at Leach
Leach Pottery: 1964 to 2005
Lives/works in St Ives, Cornwall, UK

'Without those years of making standard ware I would not have achieved the skill I now have. It became a natural ability to make and apply the right handle to a pot.'

Trevor Corser

Trevor Corser started working at the Leach Pottery in 1964, combining his work as a fisherman (crayfish diving) with his job as an odd job man at the Leach Pottery. When the weather was bad he was at the pottery mixing the clay, glazes, packing pots, stacking and firing the kiln with Bernard Leach pots and learning various skills from the different potters who were there at the time. Eventually he became a full-time apprentice, learning and being taught by Bernard and Janet Leach and Bill Marshall.

After the death of Bernard Janet gradually dispensed with the responsibility of having more students. Bill Marshall had already left to set up his own pottery, and for some years, only Trevor and Janet remained to carry on the working life of the pottery, each engaged in making pots in their own personal style and character. Janet had her wheel in the pottery cottage and Trevor in the workshop.

During those years, as well as keeping the pottery operational, Trevor assisted Janet by wedging her clay, mixing her glazes, and firing most of her pots in the big gas fired kiln. He also opened the pottery showroom to visitors. In spite of carrying out these functions to support Janet, he carried on making his own distinctive pots, mixing the glazes

Above left:
Bottle with lugs, Hakeme glaze, stoneware

Above right:
Cut sided vase, tenmoku glaze 58cm high

from powder and experimenting with ash glazes and colours. He has now given up using the old kick wheel and moved on to an electric wheel.

Trevor enjoys the whole process of working with clay and handling pots. One of the pleasures is packing and firing the kiln and looking forward to the magical moment of opening the kiln door after a firing to experience the end result.

He still uses Bernard's tools. 'I also make various tools for use in decoration from bundles of bamboo, brought by visiting Japanese potters.' They also bring gifts of brushes. A constant stream of visitors come from all over the world to see the historic collection of Leach and Hamada pots and to buy the present-day work from the pottery showroom.

Trevor Corser was the first potter to be invited to provide 'in use' pots for the Tate Gallery, St Ives, when it opened in 1993.

Making pots has been Trevor's way of life. 'I will continue to work as long as I can, because I enjoy it.' It was therefore a sad day for Trevor when in 2005, after 40 loyal years at the Leach Pottery, the workshop was closed for major refurbishment.

Antony Burgess

Born: Ramsgate, Kent 1931-2003
Studied: Travelled extensively Europe, America
Leach Pottery: 1965-1967
Lived/worked in New South Wales, Australia

'The experience of working at the Leach Pottery has stayed with me all these years'

Tony Burgess

Tony Burgess, after gaining experience by travelling in America, Canada and Mexico, returned to England in 1963 and helped John Reeve and Warren MacKenzie to start a pottery at Hennock in Devon. John Reeve left the Leach Pottery in 1961 (but later returned) and Warren MacKenzie was on a year's sabbatical from America, having previously studied with Bernard from 1949-1952.

In 1965, on the recommendations of Reeve and MacKenzie, Tony began his training at the Leach Pottery. 'I remember clearly nights spent having dinner with Bernard overlooking Porthmeor beach, talking the night away - not just about pots. What a lovely, lovely man he was.' Tony remembers all those long nights firing the second chamber of the old climbing kiln, with Bill Marshall, 'the real backbone of the pottery'. It was John Reeve, who first opened his eyes 'to see,' and was a positive influence in his development as a potter. Other overseas companions were Susan Smith, Tim Stampton and Jorgen Jorgensen. The visit of Shoji Hamada with his wife and daughter in 1966 was an inspiration to all those working at the St Ives Pottery at the time.

Whatever traumas were being experienced at the Leach Pottery -

Stoneware pots

whether at a personal or professional level - the kiln always got fired every three weeks. Effort and commitment from everyone involved was the secret of the team's success.

After completing his training at St Ives, Tony emigrated to Australia in the late 1960s and started the Tarrawonga Pottery, Mittagong in New South Wales. He also managed the Sturt Pottery there for one year. After many years, and a series of major life threatening illnesses, he returned to the Sturt Pottery where he rented workshop space to make pots he could live with. He abandoned the process of marking his pots with a seal or signature. 'My philosophy, if I have one, is that the work speaks for itself, that pots should be strong, generous, and full of life. That if they are not made with love, how can we expect others to love them?'

Collection of domestic range

Tim Stampton

Born: Brighton 1942.
Studied: Canterbury College of Art. 1962-65.
Leach pottery: 1965-67
Lives/works in County Donegal, Ireland

'I called into the pottery at St. Ives. There I met Bernard and the following day had tea with him. We had a long and pleasant conversation mainly about aesthetics and the Oriental approach.'

Tim Stampton

Tim Stampton moved back to England in the 1960s to study art at the Canterbury College of Art. His parents had emigrated to Canada in 1948. He was introduced to Janet Leach through an exhibition at the Craftsmen's Potters Association in Carnaby Street, London. During a vacation he visited St Ives to meet Bernard Leach. In the spring of 1965 Tim received a letter from Janet inviting him to replace North American Jack Worseldine. This invitation to work at the St. Ives pottery was a welcome surprise.

At that time the pottery had only the big climbing kiln. The routine therefore was critical. The disciplines of repetition throwing, drying, handling and glazing and having everything ready on time for the packing and firing was essential. Tim first built a small salt kiln which all members of the pottery used, including Bernard, and then supervised the building of the new oil fired kiln. During this time the pottery was visited by Hamada, and Bernard had a major Japanese exhibition.

After the years at the Leach pottery Tim returned to Canada and set up a pottery at Indian Point in Nova Scotia. Later he was invited to teach ceramics at Memorial University Newfoundland. Whilst at the University he was a Canadian representative at the World Craft Council Conference held in Dublin. Bernard was the special guest at this meeting.

In 1971 Tim returned to Britain with his young family and joined the Portsmouth Polytechnic Fine Art Department, where he worked with David Hamilton, who later became Head of Ceramics at the Royal College of Art.

The bulk of Tim's production in the 1970-1980s was still in the Leach tradition of functional ware. The desire to be an independent potter prompted him to build a traditional country pottery at the Amberley Chalk Pits Museum in West Sussex. Having achieved this successful project, he was keen to pursue his own personal creative work.

Over the last 32 years Tim's workshops and showrooms have shared space with books, paintings, rock samples, fossils, minerals and crystals. His spirituality comes from a close and harmonious relationship with nature.

Vase, stoneware, ash glaze 66cm high

Plate, stoneware, ash glaze 60cm diameter

Tim set up a studio in Graffham, with his new partner, the Irish potter Ros Harvey.

In 1989 they made a complete break from ceramics to painting and printmaking. They moved to Ireland, and converted their barns into studios and workshops. From here they illustrate books and exhibit internationally.

Denny Long (nee Johnston)

Born: Bristol
Studied: The West of England College of Art 1961-1967
Lives/works in St Ives, Cornwall, UK

'The time spent in Mashiko was invaluable to my research in ash glazes and glaze techniques, both for my own work and for my dissertation.'

Denny Long

Denny Long specialised in Ceramics, studying for a Diploma in Art and Design at the renamed Bristol Polytechnic. Bernard and Janet Leach were visiting tutors and with their help, and Denny's interest in Japanese culture and ceramics, she went to Japan during the summer of 1966.

Throughout her student days Denny was a frequent visitor to the Leach Pottery at St Ives and was able to take to Japan a letter of introduction from Bernard and Janet to Shoji Hamada, at Mashiko. As a student, she worked during her holidays to save enough money for the journey, taking a student ticket to travel across Soviet Russia and Siberia, then a passenger ship to Yokohama. Her experiences during her stay in Japan have influenced her life's practice as an artist. She has returned twice to Japan as a Zen Buddhist.

One of her major style influences from Japanese ceramics was Oribe ware, tableware used in groups. Denny translated the idea into larger slab built dishes, with strong geometric shapes, which could be displayed in combination. The inner surfaces like canvases, are coated with layers of ash glazes then reduction fired, the finished result giving a land or seascape impression. The colours are soft greens, blues, yellow ochre and rust.

Her large bowls were developed from encouragement given by the

Bowl, reduction fired stoneware 25.5cm high 50cm diameter

potter Lucie Rie, also a visiting tutor at Bristol Art College. Denny threw the bases and coiled onto these, giving a look of fragility to large stoneware forms. Denny invariably used white stoneware glazes for these bowls, which were decorated on the interior surface with fine incised lines, with an oxide introduced into the incision. Her small porcelain bowls were often thrown in two parts, the bowl and stem or foot joined with coiled porcelain. She glazed these with traditional porcelain glazes which she researched and made, such as sang de boeuf. This aspect of very large and very small is reflected in her printmaking today.

Slab dishes 30cm square,

Denny went on to a career in teaching, developing low fired stoneware techniques with on-glaze enamels and burnished inlaid red earthenware, suitable for secondary school students. In 1990 she began etching and printmaking and is now a successful printmaker, exhibiting widely. Denny was awarded an M.A. in Fine Art by the University of Plymouth at Falmouth College of Arts in 2001 and was elected a Royal West of England Academician in 2005.

'My story is rather like Bernard's in reverse, I began my creative life as a potter, then for the last fifteen years I have been a printmaker.'

SH

Sylvia Margaret Hardaker

Born: Coventry, 1930
Studied: Coventry School of Art
Leach Pottery: 1966-1968
Lives/works in Penzance, Cornwall, UK

'Bernard would often invite the students, for the evening, to talk. It was always so interesting to hear his philosophy. I always left with a feeling of peacefulness.'

Sylvia Hardaker

Sylvia Hardaker first came to an appreciation of pots, as a child, through illustrations in the Bible and she would make shapes from clay in the garden. Most of her fabric designs at art school included pots. Eventually she took evening classes in pottery and, once started, she was destined to be a potter. 'I had a Leach wheel made and converted the garden shed into a workshop.'

Sylvia knew of the Leach Pottery through discovering *A Potter's Book*. An approach to Janet Leach for advice on the best way to become a potter was well timed as one of the potters had just left. She was invited to meet Bernard for tea and to talk pots. Luckily Bernard liked the photographs of her work and her feeling for ceramics. Two weeks later she was a student at the Leach Pottery.

'It was a most rewarding time being part of the crew, seeing Janet Leach making her own very distinctive pots and watching her glaze some huge pieces.' Her experience at the Leach Pottery taught her to prepare clay, mix glazes, pack and fire the kiln through to the discipline of making standard ware. 'If pots did not meet requirements they would be thrown back in the clay bin.'

In the evenings and weekends Sylvia was encouraged to make her own pieces which Bernard would price for sale in the showroom or at the New Craftsman gallery in St Ives. Towards the end of her training she had her own individual kiln, which took weeks to fill. She then had to pack and fire the kiln herself, 'All the potters would arrive in the evening and Janet would provide a good selection of food and we'd have a party.'

From the proceeds of her sales Sylvia bought her first electric kiln and set up her own workshop, Kenilworth Pottery, near Coventry. It was one of the first craft shops in the area and for twenty years she made pots for domestic use. Her individual work was 'Kenzan' inspired and she used her own glazes. In 1983 Sylvia returned to Cornwall, and now lives in Penzance where she makes pots for her own pleasure.

Jug, stoneware 33cm high

Bottle, stoneware 30cm high

Chantal Donoyer

Born: Autun Saone et Loize, Burgundy, France 1945
Studied: Beaux-Arts, Beaune, Cote d'Or
Leach Pottery: 1967-1968
Lives/works in La Chapell-sous-Uchon, France

'The experience at the Leach Pottery gave me the opportunity to be influenced by Bernard, who came in every afternoon and by Bill Marshall, who was always there.'

Chantal Donoyer

Chantal Dunoyer was determined to study at the Leach Pottery, when she heard about the two year course from her college tutor. The reply to her application explained that they were booked up for the next ten years. She then studied with several potters, and at a firing with Anne Kjaersgaard, met the South African potter, Hyme Rabbinowitch, who put in a good word for her with Michael Cardew.

Michael had just returned from Nigeria and was writing *A Pioneer Potter.* During the period at Wenford Bridge with Cardew in Cornwall, Henry Hammond, who was teaching at Farnham Art School, Surrey, brought his students on a course, which included a visit to St Ives and Chantal joined them. A month later Janet Leach invited her to join the pottery to replace Susan Smith, who was returning to Australia. 'The experience of working at the Leach Pottery gave me the opportunity to be on the wheel eight hours or more a day, and to be surrounded by a warm and friendly group, while my failure to speak and understand English amused my colleagues and limited my appreciation of their philosophical discussions.'

The period at St Ives is among her warmest memories. 'It was during

Casserole, stoneware

the sixties, the flower power years. I was 22 and St Ives was a paradise of sand and palm trees, where everyone met the artists and the fisherman, the land and the sea. I had set off on a world tour to learn pottery, but as it turned out - I came back with a baby,'

In 1969 Chantal started a workshop at Toulongeon, in Burgundy, which is still her home. She throws simple, well-rounded, robust shapes. She uses naked clay, stone from Laborne and China clay, 'which reveal themselves as beautiful when the ashes and salt leave deposits.' The pots are wood-fired using chestnut and hornbeam - very few glazes, some slipware. Her three sons and friends help to fire the kiln.

She prepares the clay, cuts and splits the wood and has also rebuilt the house and workshops, all of which she loves doing, but swears she will one day save her energy for the wheel and the kiln. 'One makes pots and one is,' seems to be her philosophy.

Harry Isaacs

Born: Bury St Edmunds, Suffolk 1937
Studied: Holmes Road Institute, North London
Leach Pottery: 1968-1969
Lives/works in St Ives, Cornwall, UK

'My experience of being at the Leach Pottery changed my thoughts about life completely.'

Harry Isaacs

Harry Isaacs was working at an Adult Education Institute in North London when he first came to visit the Leach Pottery in St Ives. A long time friend, Trevor Corser, was working at the pottery and Harry contacted him about a summer job. Janet Leach asked Harry to write to her and was invited for an interview. As a result, he came to work at the pottery in the summer of 1967, during the break from teaching in London.

That summer was a revelation. The philosophy and ethos of the pottery, with Bill Marshall as the guiding light in the workshop, was a world away from the academic life Harry had been used to. As a trained engineer he understood the principles behind producing high quality standard ware and the need for discipline and productivity in the pottery workshop. What was so different was the feeling of being part of a family of potters whose head and inspiration was Bernard Leach.

'We worked and socialised together. People came from all over the world to be part of this unique experience and friendships were formed which have lasted right up to today.'

At the end of the summer of 1967 Harry returned to his teaching post in London. But in September of that year an exhibition of Bernard Leach's

Lidded pot

Salt glazed lidded pot

work was held at the Crane Kalman Gallery, in Kensington, London. Harry and his wife, Lynne, were invited to the private view and that evening Bernard invited Harry back to the pottery as a full time student.

In July 1968 Harry moved to St Ives, with his wife and baby son, and started work at the pottery. 'It was a real joy to be in an environment where people lived and breathed pottery. We often worked through the night when the climbing kiln was fired. Helping with the packing and preparation of the kiln was an incredible experience. To see the whole kiln go from cold to hot was awesome. To look through the bung holes to check the cones for the correct temperature was almost magical.'

Unfortunately, due to a serious back injury sustained at the pottery Harry was unable to carry on with pottery but continued to teach adult education classes, both at Camborne School of Art, in Redruth, and in St Ives for many years.

The unique experience of having coffee in the morning, sitting by the fireplace, and listening to Bernard's critique of a student's pot or telling a story is something I will never, ever, forget.'

Kenji Funaki

Born: Fujina, Shimane Prefecture, Japan, 1927
Studied: School of Education, Shimane University, Japan
Leach Pottery: 1967 & 1975
Lives/works in Shimane Prefecture, Japan

'Kenji is one of the most promising young craftsmen, already saying something fresh in a medium of lead glazed slipware.'[27]
Bernard Leach

Kenji Funaki

Kenji Funaki continues the traditions of the Fujina kilns which was founded by the Funaki family in 1764. The workshops are on the shore of Lake Shinji, near the old castle town of Matsue, Japan. Like his father, he admires English slipware and this has influenced much of his work, although he has also continued to carry on the traditions imported from Korea in earlier times. He left university to train as a potter. He studied with Hamada in 1950 and three years later he was invited to produce pottery at Okinawa, where Hamada had worked, producing pots with unique red decoration.

His father, Michitada, was a friend of Bernard Leach, who had known three generations of the Funaki family. Bernard visited the Fujina kilns at Matsue in 1934 and was there to demonstrate and help with the techniques of lead glazed English slipware, already introduced by Hamada on his return to Japan. Slip techniques were not used in traditional Japanese potteries. Leach also taught the Funakis the art of applying a handle. 'Technically, the way he made the handles of pitchers served as a good reference.'

Given these close connections it is not surprising that, 'Following the

***Left:** Jug, stoneware, with transparent glaze*

***Above:** Two Jugs, with transparent glaze*

recommendation of Mr Bernard Leach I came to England to Study pottery. I mainly trained with his eldest son David Leach in Devon.' During his 1975 stay he studied mediaeval pitchers, slipware, and the variety of ceramics in the museums. European traditions had a big impact on the Fujina kilns. In a subsequent visit to Matsue, Leach was impressed with the work of Kenji as a craftsman who was using lead-glazed slipware in Japan.

In 1986 Kenji Funaki exhibited in the Liberty 'Mingei' Exhibition in London with Tatsuzo Shimaoka and Shinsaku Hamada. Kenji's pieces were in reddish brown, a traditional colour of the Funaki kilns, with a glaze glassy and transparent, showing the slip decoration beneath, trailed and combed. He also showed Korean-style vases and jugs, plates and boldly designed dishes and tiles, decorated with paintings of fish, hens and other animals. 'I enjoy making my pots and designing my own creations. I use the seal which was designed and made by Bernard Leach.'

John Bedding

Born: London 1947
Studied: Sir John Cass School of Art, London
Leach Pottery: 1968-1971 & 1973-1978
Lives/works in St Ives, Cornwall, UK

'Bernard's biggest influence was his philosophy. He was around for my first two years. Bill Marshall was the main influence for the shape of pots. Janet looked with a sculptor's eye.'

John Bedding

John Bedding came to St Ives with Bernard's *A Potter's Book* in his hand and an intention to work at the Leach Pottery. He first worked at two local potteries until his persistence paid off and Janet Leach offered him a two-year student apprenticeship. After this he worked with Jean Tessier at his atelier in Villenaux, France. On his return Janet asked him to join the permanent staff at the pottery. During this time he was allowed to develop his own work. He had three solo exhibitions in London, Plymouth, and a farewell exhibition in the Leach Showroom before studying in Japan in 1978.

The Japanese trip was arranged through Janet and Bernard Leach, with Shigeyoshi Ichino, the eldest son of Tanso Ichino with whom Janet had studied. John spent a year in Tachiqui, a small village in the centre of Tamba, with a thousand years of tradition in pottery where they used the multi-chambered wood-fired dragon kilns. His year culminated in a sell-out solo show in Osaka.

After a brief tour of the East he returned to England and set up workshops where he worked in isolation, finding his own style, and started to experiment with low-fired techniques, including Raku, to distance himself from the Leach and Japanese influences. 'I was torn between my love for traditional stoneware pottery and my desire to experiment with the chemistry of ceramics. The ground-breaking work had been done over years of tradition and the glazes and techniques could not be bettered.'

In 1990 John moved his workshop to St Ives and on the same premises opened 'St Ives Ceramics,' a specialist gallery showing the best studio pottery from around the world. A proportion of the work is from former Leach students, or from potters influenced by the Leach tradition.

John has since opened and is working in 'Gaolyard Studios,' a group of nine purpose- built pottery studios. Although the potters work as individuals, much of the communal flavour of the old Leach Pottery exists, with potters working in harmony, sharing ideas and over-coming problems. 'It is the modern day answer to the lack of working potteries, like the Leach, that aspiring potters need for their growth.'

A further commitment John has made to the Leach memory is in joining a group dedicated to its preservation and in bringing the pottery into public ownership. John is a founder director of the charity Bernard Leach (St Ives) Trust.

Above: *Squared earthenware pot*

Right: *Ceramic ring*

AB

Alan Brough

Born: Wilmslow, Cheshire, 1924
Studied: Camberwell School of Arts and Crafts
Leach Pottery: 1968-1972
Lives/works in Newlyn, Cornwall UK

'Bernard said that a good pot would look equally well on an old piece of furniture as it would on a modern Swedish glass table.'

Alan Brough

Alan Brough, already a very experienced potter, went to the Leach Pottery to help organise the students. Bill Marshall was working with Bernard,who was in his eighties, helping to throw his large pots, and Janet wanted someone to organise the workshops. As well as doing this, Alan was making his own pots in his particular style and encouraging the students to find theirs. His son Adrian is also a potter.

When he left in 1972 he started the Alan Brough Pottery in nearby Newlyn, and was there for 18 years, making stoneware and porcelain. 'Now I am older I'm making earthenware. Bernard was a glaze man. I am a form and decorative man.' He used to dine with Bernard quite regularly and learned to listen and adapt, not to follow. He felt others made pale imitations of Leach pots and therefore failed in finding themselves.

'Bernard made very important statements, he said, "If you want to make a soup bowl think soup." If Alan makes a vessel for water or wine it will look right for the liquid it will hold. He learnt to think usefulness and suitability. 'Bernard pointed out that if an Indian woman was going to make a bowl for wheat she would make a low shallow dish for that

purpose. She would do it without intellectualising. He thought some of the best pots were made by women.'

Alan tells his students the potentialities of clay, which is for him the most important material in the world, encouraging them to explore the particular clay in their area and decide whether to study glazes, or make sculptural forms, or pure potters' forms for use. 'I wouldn't like to tell anybody what kind of pots to make.' He feels clay has become invisible because of its usefulness. 'Some of the history of the world is written on so-called stones, which were really clay slabs fired.' He makes pots because he wants clay to be visible.

In France, where he has exhibited, he finds a great acceptance of red earthenware and a high regard and deep feeling for the craft of pottery. 'There the craftsman is valued and enjoys a dignified status.'

In 2005, at 80 years old, he still attends his studio for three to four hours a day making slab pots in porcelain and stoneware to suit modern living and architectural innovation, without forgetting his first love of thrown forms.

Porcelain vases, copper red, orange over wax decoration blue ying ching 23cm high

Vase, stoneware, green ying ching, painted wax decoration 44cm high

Shigeyoshi Ichino

Born: Tachikui, Tamba, Japan 1942
Studied: Kansai University Economy Faculty
Leach Pottery: 1969-1973
Lives/works in Hyogoken, Japan

'I came to learn how to put a handle on pitchers and pots and how to paint on pottery in the Bernard Leach way.'

Shigeyoshi Ichino

Shigeyoshi Ichino began a tour of Europe with a year of study with Bernard and Janet Leach. He is the eldest son of Japanese potter Tanso Ichino of Tamba. In the early1950s Janet had been welcomed to the mountain village of Tamba by the Ichino family, where she spent several months perfecting her pots. The invitation for a son of the Ichino family to come to St Ives returned the courtesy and kindness shown to her during her stay in Japan. In St Ives Shigeyoshi passed on his knowledge of potting in the Japanese style and exhibited his work at the Penwith Gallery, St Ives.

In Britain Shigeyoshi relished the multitude of museums and galleries in which to see collections of ceramics and other art treasures. London was a convenient starting point for a European tour and in 1971 he was in Villenaux, France, where he directed the construction of a kiln for Atelier du Cep and renewed his friendship with John Bedding with whom he had studied at the Leach Pottery. They exhibited together in a group exhibition at a local gallery in Villenaux.

In 1973 he held his first one-man exhibition at Kotokan Museum in Tamba, simultaneously he exhibited in a solo show at the Turret Bookshop Gallery, London. On his return to Japan he exhibited frequently in

one-man shows in Osaka and Tokyo and most recently in both cities. For several years the Daimaru Department Store in Kobe, has held 'father and Son' exhibitions. In 1981 Shigeyoshi exhibited with Janet Leach at the Amalgam Art Gallery, London. After being appointed lecturer at the National Hyogo University of Education, Japan, a great opportunity to revisit Britain came with the invitation in1988 to stage a one-man exhibition in Dundee, Scotland, as part of the 'Japan Fair,' sponsored by the City of Dundee.

His work ethic is to blend traditional methods into contemporary pottery using Tamba-Yaki firing techniques, based on Rokkohu of Japan. He especially loves to throw large plates, using traditional skills, and decorating with salt glazes and slip. 'I make pots I can enjoy using in every day life. I never become tired of them.' He continues the seven-hundred year history of pottery making in his village in Tamba.

Traditional Tamba style wood-fired bottle

Diamond shaped bottle vase

J.O

Jeff Oestreich

Born: St Paul, Minnesota, USA 1947
Studied: Art and Art History, University of Minnesota
Leach Pottery: 1969-1971
Lives/works in Minnesota, USA

'Working at the Leach Pottery had many meanings. It provided a structure to integrate pottery making with life. I am grateful for that opportunity to focus so intensely on potting.'

Jeff Oestreich

Jeff Oestreich knew of Bernard Leach through *A Potter's Book*. The ideas and philosophy expressed in that book rang a bell for him and he decided to forward his pottery studies outside of the university system. To this end he travelled to St Ives for an interview with Bernard Leach on the recommendation of Warren MacKenzie and, having been accepted, returned the following year to begin his training as an apprentice. 'To be part of a family that was passionate about clay was a gift to me.'

Life and pottery became inseparable. His sole purpose was to learn through the daily making of pots to become a skilled potter. This he achieved, and set up his studio in America upon his return in 1971, working in porcelain and stoneware. 'The practice and philosophy of the Leach Pottery instilled in me a work ethic which has continued throughout my life.'

All Jeff's work is wheel-thrown on an adaptation of a Leach wheel. His original commitment to utility is still important to him, although there are times when ideas override strict function and the pots may challenge the user. He often finds these pots are successful, and they lead to further investigations with thrown and altered forms. Throughout his potting life

he has retained his attachment to a colour palette of Japanese and Chinese glazes. At his workshop at Taylors Falls, Minnesota, he is presently exploring glazes in bands of green, turquoise and grey.

A major catalyst for change has been the exploration of a variety of firing methods, from electric and gas to a salt kiln, but he confesses to a romantic attachment to wood-burning kilns which remind him of St Ives. They require help from friends and therefore fulfil a social function, although the work is exhausting. It also means a search for glazes that will flux in the cooler areas.

Vase

His experiences have led him to believe that variety and challenge are elements that keep alive interest in clay. 'The challenge of making work that functions on both a visual and physical level remains a consuming interest.' In 1995 Jeff was artist-in-residence at Unitec, Auckland, New Zealand. A return visit in 2005 confirmed that 'Leach had a huge influence on their pottery movement years ago.'

Boat, soda fired 40.5cm long

Peter Hardy

Born: St Ives, Cornwall 1950
Studied: High Wycombe College of Art, Ceramics
Leach Pottery: 1971-1973
Lives/works in St Buryan, Cornwall, UK

'Bernard's teaching made me aware of form and the subtleties of detail, and I still feel his presence while I am working'

Peter Hardy

Peter Hardy was born in St Ives and spent his formative years there. He attended school with the children of artists Patrick Heron, Bill Redgrave, Robin Nance, Barbara Hepworth and Terry Frost.

He became interested in pottery at school in Penzance. While studying pottery at art school he asked Janet Leach for the plans to build a Leach kick wheel. She sold him a second hand wheel and offered him a vacation job. He subsequently left art school and joined the crew at the pottery, throwing on the wheel previously occupied by Jeff Oestreich, opposite Bill Marshall.

At first he made the simpler items of standard ware as well as learning to mix clay and fire the big oil fired kilns. Trevor took him under his wing, showing him the basic principles of kiln stacking and firing. Firing the climbing kiln was a procedure that involved the whole group, Bill Marshall, Alan Brough, Trevor, Shigeyoshi Ichino, and John Bedding. This was the era of big kilns and the last few times the climbing kiln was fired using oil and side- stoking with wood.

'The end of the sixties and the beginning of the seventies were exciting times at the pottery. Bernard would come and make pots and keep in

Caddy & cheese dish

touch and offer helpful criticism of our efforts.' The group were encouraged to make their own work, using the kilns which had been built by previous students. 'Needless to say, my own efforts at this time were pretty dire. I was the youngest student and much in awe of the older more experienced potters.'

Jug 22cm high

Peter learnt from working at the pottery; far more than any art school could have taught him. Making pottery is still an important part of his life and, 'I am grateful that Bernard and Janet were so patient and generous in giving me the opportunity to work and learn alongside them.' He keeps in touch with Bill Marshall and helps to fire his kiln at Lelant when necessary.

Peter has lived near the village of St Buryan since 1987 and makes pots in the converted farm buildings on the property. He uses his old kick wheel and various kilns. He is a member of Cornwall Crafts, selling his work through their galleries. He concentrates mainly on high-fired stoneware and porcelain, enjoying getting to grips with clay and fire.

Michael Cartwright

Born: Sawston, South Cambridgeshire, 1951
Studied: Ceramics at Farnham School of Art, Surrey
Leach Pottery: 1973-1975
Lives/works in Kingsbridge, Devon, UK

'Living and working with people for whom pot making sustained their very existence was a revelation.

Michael Cartwright

Michael Cartwright was introduced to ceramics on the foundation course at Cambridge College of Art and Technology. His lecturer, Zoe Ellison, inspired him sufficiently for him to change his course from painting to studying ceramics at Farnham College of Art, Surrey. On finishing his course the ultimate goal was to work at the Leach Pottery. Few workshops offered training or apprenticeships at that time.

He knew Cornwall well, having spent previous summers helping to fire Michael Cardew's wood burning kiln at Wenford Bridge. He approached Janet Leach but there were no places available at that time. He worked as a technician on the Studio Pottery course at Harrow School of Art, Middlesex, the year Mick Casson left. When Shigeyoshi Ichino left the Leach Pottery to return to Japan, Michael was pleased to be offered the vacated space in the workshop. 'It was at St Ives that I felt I did some of my best ceramic work. A taste for pots that are unpretentious was acquired at this time and remains until the present day. I admire pots that are about weight, comfort and quietness whilst remaining strong and personal.'

After eighteen very enjoyable months he prepared to set up his own pottery in Cambridge. Spike Pottery, where he produced a standard ware

Tea set (earthenware)

range and some individual pieces, was in existence for four years. He also lectured in ceramics. Whilst in St Ives he had taken up surfing and was desperately missing the sea. This desire to live in a marine environment led to a move to the Guernsey Pottery in the Channel Islands. He trained a team of proficient throwers, helping switch production from slip cast to thrown ware, and redesigning a stoneware and earthenware range.

A career change took him to Reading University to study as a secondary school teacher. He took a job at Ivybridge Community College in South Devon, where he teaches art and ceramics to 11 to 18 year old students.

More recently, Michael has participated in several group and one-man exhibitions showing his drawings and paintings that relate to that ever-present passion for the sea. He retains an interest in ceramics and feels Bernard's concern with form, particularly in relation to standard ware, has not really been matched by many contemporary studio potters.

Teapots 2 pint. Slip decorated earthenware. Kaki glazed stoneware

Ian Box

Born: Fulham, London 1949
Studied: Ceramics at Cornwall College
Leach Pottery: 1974-1975
Lives/works in Sennen, Cornwall, UK

'The experience of working at the Leach Pottery was of enormous benefit to me. At first I felt overawed,but the camaraderie of my workmates soon put me at ease.'

Ian Box

Ian Box moved to Cornwall in 1957 with his mother and twin brother. In 1972 with his wife and brother, he studied ceramics at Cornwall College under Roger Veal and David Metcalfe. William Marshall was introduced in 1973 to teach throwing techniques and Janet Leach was the course advisor. On seeing his diploma presentation Janet invited him to work for her at the Leach Pottery. He also gained Licentiate acceptance of the Society of Industrial Artists and Designers.

Bill Marshall's enthusiasm and love of pottery were an inspiration. Ian found the potters working at Leach – Trevor Corser, John Bedding, John Reeve and Mick Cartwright – extremely capable and immersed himself in the task of becoming as able as them. His throwing technique improved considerably. 'The experience gave me the precious gifts of enthusiasm and confidence in my ability and for that I am very grateful.' Janet Leach worked at her wheel in the pottery cottage but was in regular contact. 'She was very aware of my progress, guiding me where she could.'

After leaving the Leach Pottery he and his wife started the Trevillian Pottery in Penzance. After five years, he then worked as a technician at Falmouth School of Art and finally in 1984 became a Day Care Officer at

Coffee pot and bowl, wax resist, stoneware. Plate 28cm diameter

the John Daniel Centre in Penzance, where he teaches pottery and social skills. He works with low-fired terracotta ware, which students can decorate. 'Teaching pottery to people with learning difficulties needs small steps, and sees small achievements. For twenty-two years this has been a learning experience for me. The work of the potter is both a mental and a spiritual process; to succeed one must have love and determination.'

Chun water jug, ash glazed stoneware 28cm high

On occasions Ian and his wife visited Bernard at his flat at Barnaloft. 'I will never forget Bernard, when he was 90 and blind, he picked up a bowl from a shelf and asked me, "Where do you think it was made?" My answer was to use logic and guess Japan. He replied, "No, it is from Korea; a bowl I really love – you can feel it." He had a spiritual awareness and love of the ceramic craft and stood out as a beacon in the twentieth century.'

'Although I hoped to build a reduction stoneware kiln at my home in Sennen, I have had to shelve this due to other priorities. Other projects have occupied my time, but I still hope to build a new kiln one day.'

William Klock

Born: Orwigsburg, Pennsylvania , USA 1933
Studied: Fine Art, Ceramics,
New York University
Leach Pottery 1975-1976
Lives/works in Morrisonville,
New York, USA

'During my lifetime there have been few events more important than my year at the Leach Pottery. My experiences have left an indelible imprint on my work in clay and as a teacher of ceramics.'

William Klock

William Klock began his interest in clay in America by way of Bernard Leach's *A Potter's Book*. He had written letters to Leach over several years indicating his interest in studying with him. Finally, his wish was fulfilled by an invitation from Janet Leach to come to St Ives for an interview. At this point he was already an established potter teaching studio pottery at a University in the USA. He arrived with his wife and three young sons and took a house in Hellesvean. 'Rosedale' was of particular importance because it had one of Bernard's ceramic horses attached to the ridge tiles.

One of the great lessons learned by William at the Leach Pottery and emphasized by both Bill Marshall and Bernard Leach in their discussions of pots, was the importance of simplicity and directness of execution within the limitations of the clays, glazes and the kiln; never force an outcome. He has a wood-fired kiln but does not fire often. His workshop routine and studio equipment are similar to that of the Leach Pottery. 'One could say my mentality in clay really developed there.'

Consequently, William has pursued an economy-of-means approach with materials and firing. He works primarily in stoneware, limiting himself to a few slips and glazes to get the most from the least. His work develops in series, permitting him to make visual comparisons and decisions, whereby a progression occurs by which ideas and forms take on subtle meaning and importance.

Bernard's descriptions of Korean ceramics, and why he considered them monumental and how they had influenced his theories of form, were so intriguing that in 1989 William went to Korea to live and work with Korean craftsmen. He discovered the Onggi potters, who made utilitarian ware ranging in size from small to very large pots that require considerable strength and concentration. Since his return to the States he has lectured and written articles on Korean Onggi and realised the Korean roots in his own work.

William was awarded the title of Professor Emeritus, State University of New York. He and his wife run a studio/showroom in upstate New York, near Plattsburgh. The Klocks, Bill and Anna, return every few years to St Ives and take a special interest in the pottery as a vital factor in the historic and ongoing development of ceramics for future generations.

Pot, copper red glaze, 24cm high

Vase, saturated copper glaze, stamped sponge impressions 56cm high

RFP

Robert Fishman

Born: Province, Rhode Island, USA 1951
Studied: Rhode Island College, Ceramics
Leach Pottery: 1976-1978
Lives/works in Rhode Island, USA

'The lessons, information and skills I was taught and allowed to hone while at the Leach Pottery are priceless.'

Robert Fishman

Robert Fishman made his first trip to Europe after graduating from college. It was always his goal to visit the Leach Pottery and on arriving Janet Leach showed him around. He was very impressed with what he saw. A few months after returning to America Janet telephoned to offer a two-year apprenticeship. 'Being able to work in an environment with Bill Marshall, John Bedding and Trevor Corser and others, especially with the guidance of Janet, and visiting Bernard on a weekly basis and have him handle my pottery was inspiring.' At the time Bernard was writing his final book *Beyond East and West* and Robert was able to read it back to him after his secretary had typed it.

Back in America Robert met Harry and Elizabeth Spring who were running a successful pottery and he took a job throwing for them. He identified and developed a line of suitable functional ware. In 1980 he set up a studio where Harry helped build his first kiln. Soon he was employing seven people but fearing he was becoming more manager than potter, he built another, smaller pottery in Rhode Island with the help of one man, who worked with him for fifteen years.

Robert developed distinctive and decorative, hand-painted brushwork

Cannister set, hand painted blue and white

on his pots. He tries to identify and keep in touch with trends in the areas where he sells his pots. The present colours are blue and white. 'I believe that's what sells my pottery. The decoration and the colours I choose. I don't think I am compromising in any way. Janet used to say, "Make sure the tail doesn't wag the dog." I always try to keep this in the back of my mind.'

Bath set, hand painted blue and white

All Robert's pots are thrown on the wheel. He fires in an electric kiln in an oxidising atmosphere where he has control over the colours. He does not make one-off pieces. His goal is to achieve a body of work that will take a lifetime to fulfil and to make good functional pots that people can live with and enjoy. 'It takes a lot of hours to become a potter but you can't count the hours.'

Jeffrey D. Larkin

Born: Minnesota 1950
Studied: University of Minnesota, ceramics
Leach Pottery: 1976-1978
Lives/Works: Featherstone Pottery, Minnesota, USA

'Something was going right at the Leach Pottery and I knew I wanted to experience it for myself'

Jeff Larkin

Jeff Larkin was inspired by the work and teaching of Warren MacKenzie at the University of Minnesota ceramics programme. Jeff came to appreciate the tradition of the Leach Pottery through Warren and his experience at the Leach Pottery. He read in-depth Bernard Leach's *A Potter's Book* which described a concept that intrigued him, that of a pottery as a workshop. He also read about the work of Bill Marshall and his teaching, and having seen some of his pots that were brought back from St Ives Jeff wanted to acquire the same skills he felt could be achieved in a working pottery.

In 1976 Jeff was accepted to work at the Leach Pottery. His first role was to learn the complexity of mixing various clay bodies and other odd jobs involved in the day-to-day pottery business. Soon he was assigned a wheel and under Bill Marshall's tutelage, learned the process of repetitive throwing by making standard ware, and developed an eye for good pots versus bad pots.

Having a British heritage, Jeff travelled the country to absorb information, not only about the pottery industry, but the British culture as well. A once in a lifetime opportunity was given to him to go ferret hunting with fellow Leach potter and friend, Trevor Corser.

Upon Jeff's return to Minnesota in 1978, he put into action his plans to establish a studio on the 150 year old ancestral farm, that is, the birthplace of his mother, Alice Featherstone Larkin. For years he had been intrigued with the wood fired pottery process and he enlisted the skills of his father, a bricklayer and stonemason, and together with his brothers constructed a 30 foot, four chamber wood-fired climbing kiln. The adjacent chicken house was renovated into a studio and evolved into what is today known as, Featherstone Pottery.

Jeff maintains a partnership with his brother, Tom, and together they produce functional wood-fired stoneware and porcelain items utilizing local raw materials for clay body and glazes.

Other persons working with Jeff at the Leach Pottery were Bernard and Janet Leach, Bill Marshall, Trevor Corser, Zelia Vandenberg, Willie Klock, Robert Fishman, John Bedding and Jason Wason.

Assorted dishes

Two jars, stoneware

Jason Wason

Born: Liverpool 1946
Studied: Ceramics, self taught. Travelled extensively, Asia, North Africa, Middle East
Leach Pottery: 1976-1981
Lives/works in St Just, Cornwall, UK

"The Leach Pottery functioned really well because all the technical problems had been ironed out over a good many years.'

Jason Wason

Jason Wason joined the Leach Pottery in 1976. It was then a group of eight, with Bill Marshall as head potter, Janet Leach working in her own studio and Bernard in semi-retirement, concentrating on his writing. Each person was responsible for a given number of functional shapes, mugs, jugs, bowls, casseroles, etc. which were part of the standard domestic ware collection. As the individual's skill grew they moved along to tackle the more complex shapes. 'I greatly valued the repetition throwing, partly as a way of improving skills on the wheel, but also as a way of developing the eye to the subtle variations of form.' His apprenticeship gave him a strong sense of workshop discipline and technical competence but allowed him the freedom to experiment and develop his own designs.

'Although many students have passed through the Leach there is an immediate recognition of those people, something which is hard to explain, but it has to do with the construction of a pot, the way the foot relates to the shoulder, the neck and so on.'

Jason set up his own workshop in 1981 and lives with his wife Joanna, also a potter, on the wild moorland near St Just, West Cornwall, between Geevor and Pendeen tin mines. From his studio window he has panoramic views over the Atlantic Ocean out towards the Isles of Scilly. The landscape is rich in mineral deposits from former mine workings that find their way into the work in one way or another.

He tends not to use orthodox glazes but instead explores the texture of the clay itself. Surface colour comes from a variety of methods, including the use of sawdust or straw firings, oxides, raku or other post-firing processes, depending on what aspect of the pot he is trying to emphasise. Jason's work is not a production range of pre-designed pottery, but an ongoing experimental investigation into surface and texture, and an exploration of the subtleties of form that define the character of each individual piece. His love of clay and the alchemical processes involved in the firings still excite him enough to maintain the momentum to experiment. His lifelong travel bug has not subsided, so he has readily accepted offers to be 'Artist in Residence' in Japan twice, and visiting lecturer in Jerusalem and Tel Aviv.

His work is regularly represented by Austin Desmond Fine Art, London. He has also exhibited in Santa Fe, Chicago, Dublin, Amsterdam and Tokyo. His work is in permanent collections, including the Boymans Van Beuningen Museum, Rotterdam, Holland, The Togei Messe Museum, Mashiko, Japan and the British High Commission, Dhakar, Bangladesh.

Lidded pot 18cm high

Gold and green vessel 40cm high

Nic Harrison

Born: London 1949
Studied: Studio Pottery Course, Cornwall College
Leach Pottery: 1979-1980
Works in Helston, Cornwall, UK

'An important time at the Leach was spent in the pot room with the collection of Hamada, Cardew, Hans Coper, Lucy Rie and Bernard Leach, to give inspiration'

Nic Harrison

Nic Harrison moved to Cornwall with his wife Jackie in 1975. At the time of his studies in Studio Pottery at Cornwall College, Bill Marshall was a lecturer while both Henry Hammond and Janet Leach were external assessors. Nic responded to Bill's contagious enthusiasm and love of his craft. 'Bill often waxed lyrical about clay, glazes, pots and all aspects of the craft.' When Nic completed the course, he was invited by Janet to join the Leach Pottery. Although Janet was away much of the time in Japan with various exhibitions of Bernard's work, when she was available at the pottery she proved to be a strict, though kindly, disciplinarian. Nic was the last student taken on at the Leach Pottery in 1979, the year Bernard died.

He worked as part of the team which included Trevor Corser and Jason Wason and was involved in producing a portion of the standard ware: soup bowls with lids, small tankards, plates, sugar bowls and egg cups. He took part in all aspects of working in a studio pottery, from clay preparation, throwing and glazing to firing the kiln. He also assisted in selling from the showroom and displaying exhibitions at the Penwith Gallery, St Ives.

Bowl, porcelain
12cm diameter

Vase, stoneware

Nic remembers the room in the Cottage, overlooking the garden at the pottery, which contained the "pots of inspiration". It was a collection of pots to which the potters had access, in order to seek inspiration and experience moments of contemplation.

When Nic moved on to set up his own pottery workshop, he carried the influence of the Leach collection of pots with him. He found it almost impossible to work in any other way but The Leach Tradition: 'It is a way of life; always finding new ways to extend the experience.'

The Vyvyan family offered workshop space in the old stable courtyard at Trelowarren House near Helston. In 1981, Nic with wife Jackie, a weaver, opened a gallery and studios on the estate. In 2005 they moved to their new gallery, Nic Harrison Ceramics in Helston. He produces an extensive range of domestic stoneware and porcelain pottery. He worked originally on a Leach kick wheel, but now uses an electric wheel, using Dobles, St Agnes stoneware clay. He uses Tenmoku, Celadon and Ying Ching glazes, the traditional glazes of the Leach Pottery. Decoration is achieved by applying oxides of cobalt, iron, manganese or copper to the glaze surface. In true Leach tradition of 'flowing through' the whole process' Nic has designed and built his own reduction fired kilns, which are fired with propane gas. 'The learning never stops.'

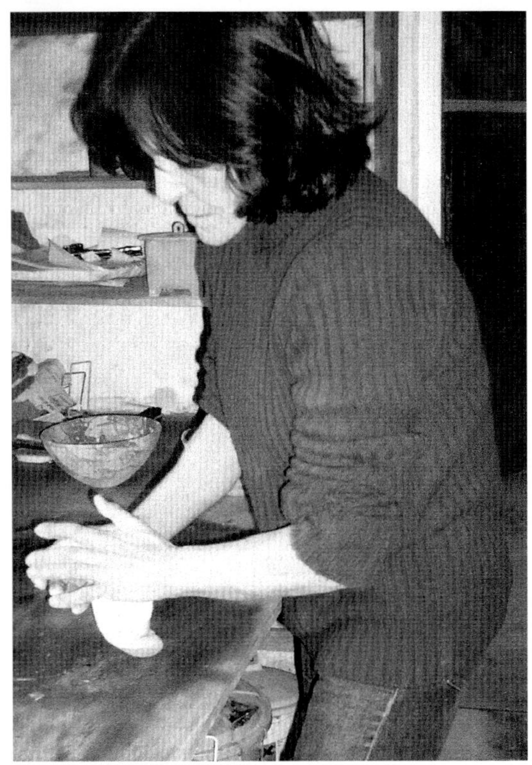

Joanna Wason

Born: Berlin 1952, grew up in Bideford, Devon, UK
Studied: Fine Art at Exeter and Liverpool Art Schools. BA Hons. OU
Leach Pottery: 1988 to 2005
Lives in St Just, Cornwall, UK

'I always found conversations with Janet Leach interesting, and often extremely entertaining, whether about pots or her life with Bernard.'

Joanna Wason

Joanna Wason, living in Bideford, North Devon, always admired the old collection of local honey-glaze slipware harvest jugs, displayed in tall glass cases, in Bideford Museum. These traditional jugs were decorated with farming and sea-going images scratched into the slip. There was no artificial finesse about these generously proportioned, friendly pots.

The first time Joanna worked with clay was in Scotland in 1974 where her husband Jason and two other potters set up a pottery workshop. While the others made pots, Joanna made figurative sculptures, later learning mould-making techniques and experimenting with other materials.

Moving back to St Just, in the West Country, Jason went to work at the Leach Pottery, while Jo divided her time between bringing up their sons, and casual work on farms, waitressing and gardening, but she continued making clay portrait sculptures and life-sized animal garden sculptures, having seen old examples in reclamation yards. She made various figurative items including water spouts for gutters, memories of the gargoyles at New College, Oxford, which she had seen as a teenager.

In 1988 Janet Leach asked Jo to come and help her in her workshop at the Leach Pottery, preparing clay, mixing glazes, making saggars for Bizen smoke firings and helping with her particular firing methods. Jo continued to work for her throughout Janet's final nine highly productive years, which ended with a sell-out show of new pots in London a matter of months before she died.

'In Pottery Cottage there was an impressive collection of very fine pots made by leading 20th century western potters, such as Lucie Rie and Maria Martinez, as well as ancient and modern Japanese pots, and ancient Chinese and Korean pots.' This collection filled the room where Joanna wrote letters to Janet's wide circle of (often potters, sometimes eminent) friends, to her dictation.

Since Janet's death, Jo has stayed at the Leach Pottery making pots, boxes, bowls, and bottles for the showroom. She works in stoneware, thrown or hand-built, with iron-rich glazes and ash glazes which she particularly likes, partly because of its ancient and accidental origins (glaze being created incidentally by 'fly ash' in early, very hot, Oriental kilns) and partly because, being a gardener, she enjoys the strange process of transforming the residue of clearance bonfires into something beautiful by firing it up once more, this time as glaze, in the gas kiln at the pottery.

Joanna was still working at the Leach Pottery in 2005 before the workshop closed down for major refurbishment.

Tea bowl 8cm and vase

Bottle, ash glaze 40cm high

Tomoo Hamada

Born: Mashiko, Japan 1967
Studied: Graduate and Post Graduate art, Tama University
Leach Pottery: 1995
Lives/works in Mashiko, Japan

'I was told the story of St Ives and Bernard Leach by my grandmother and my father almost daily.'

Tomoo Hamada

Tomoo Hamada remembers the international atmosphere surrounding his grandfather, Shoji Hamada, even when he was at primary school. St Ives was the most familiar place for him in England and when Tomoo had the opportunity to visit in 1995 he felt it was the chance of a lifetime. 'I wanted to investigate and reconfirm the relationships between Bernard and Shoji.' At the Leach Pottery Tomoo was impressed by a potters wheel designed by Bernard Leach; an improved version of the kick wheel. He was looking at what is known as the 'Modified Leach Pottery Wheel.' He hoped the climbing kiln, sadly no longer used, would be preserved, but was relieved to find the Leach Pottery still functioning, with Janet Leach and Trevor Corser still potting, alongside a collection of Leach pottery.

His father, Shinsaku, had also visited St Ives Pottery and afterwards had accompanied Shoji, acting as his assistant, on a lecture tour of America. Kazue, his grandmother, came to St Ives in 1966.

After finishing his university studies, Tomoo decided to join his father, Shinsaku, at the Mashiko pottery. He works with him, enjoying the family traditions and values, but at the same time exploring and creating works that are entirely Tomoo, and different from Shinsaku, Atsuya and from

Shoji - a difficult task when preceded by three master potters of the same family.

'I make pots in tune with the rotation of the kick wheel. The process of work from the start to the completion should be done with spontaneous rhythm. I use natural glaze and fire them in a kiln with pine wood. These processes provide the pots with the atmosphere of nature.' In 1995 he exhibited at Togami Gallery in Yamagata City, before coming to Britain. 'St Ives is a beautiful town with blue skies and sea, bright and peaceful. I hope to develop relationships between St Ives and Mashiko.'

With the recent Heritage grants to the Leach Pottery, Tomoo's hoped for wish between St Ives and Mashiko is likely to take place, the Japanese being especially connected, and interested, in the Leach Pottery.

Vase, white glaze, green and red enamel over-glaze

Teapot and cups, copper and white glaze, painted green and red, enamel over-glaze

Amanda Brier

Born: Portsmouth 1978
Studied: Ceramics, Falmouth College of Arts
Leach Pottery: 2000 to present day
Lives in Falmouth, Cornwall, UK

'My work is mostly inspired by the combination of Bernard Leach's decoration and the fine, light, delicate porcelain pots by David Leach.'

Amanda Brier

Amanda Brier decided to write to the Leach Pottery, after graduating in Studio Ceramics at Falmouth College of Arts, and enquire into any position that might be available. Throughout her degree she was one of a small group of students who shared an interest in the work of Bernard Leach and potters working in the Leach tradition. 'Writing to the Leach Pottery seemed the first obvious step for me to take.'

Three months after graduating she was employed at the pottery by the current owner Alan Gillam. Her first job was to catalogue the pots that made up the exhibition situated on the ground floor of what was the Leach pottery cottage. Being able to handle and photograph pots by Bernard Leach, Shoji Hamada, David Leach, Janet Leach and many others allowed her to absorb their form, proportion, weight, glaze and decoration, which was an interesting and inspiring start to her time at the pottery.

Amanda was then invited to join Joanna Wason and Trevor Corser in the pottery, making pots to sell on site in the showroom. She had not yet really developed her own style of work and spent many months continuing glaze experiments started at college, and throwing new forms,

Collection of porcelain pots, trinket box, fluted mug, bowl, fluted jug

making bowls, jugs, vases, mugs and practising applying handles.

'Surrounded by Leach pots and working in this eighty four year old pottery, throwing on a kick wheel and using Leach glaze recipes has had an enormous influence on my work.'

In 2001, as well as working at the Leach Pottery, Amanda set up her own pottery where she lives in Falmouth. With help from The Prince's Trust she was able to buy a wheel and kiln and started to make work to sell in local galleries and at fairs around the country. She hand paints tiles and pots with animals, mainly fish and birds, and stylised floral designs.

Stoneware vase with olive green glaze. Height 21 cms

'I feel privileged for having the chance to experience working in such an historic pottery and to be involved in so many aspects of working at the pottery, knowing and becoming friends with members of the Leach family and potters associated with this legacy. It has been the most fantastic start to what I hope will be a long career as a studio potter.'

Amanda was still working at the Leach Pottery in 2005 before the workshop closed down for major refurbishment.

The Leach Potters

Potters Profiled	Dates at the Pottery
BERNARD LEACH	1920-1979
SHOJI HAMADA	1920-1923
DAVID LEACH	1930-1955
JANET LEACH	1956-1997

Students and Apprentices	
MICHAEL CARDEW	1923-1926
KATHARINE PLEYDELL-BOUVERIE	1924-1925
NORAH BRADEN	1924-1927
CHARLOTTE EPTON	1927-1930
BERNARD FORRESTER	1932-1933
HARRY & MAY DAVIS	1933-1937
DOUGLAS ZADEK	1936-1938
MARSHALL WILLIAM	1938-1977
DOROTHY KEMP	1939-1945
MARGARET LEACH	1941-1945
ROBERT LOUIS BLATHERWICK	1942-1943
MICHAEL GILL	1943
DONALD MILLS	1944
MARY GIBSON-HORROCKS	1944-1947
VALERIE BOND	1945-1946
KENNETH QUICK	1945-1955 & 1960-1963
GUTTE ERIKSEN	1948
CECIL BAUGH	1948-1950
GEOFFREY WHITING	1949 Visitor
WARREN & ALIX MACKENZIE	1949-1952
VALENTINOS CHARALAMBOUS	1950-1951
MICHAEL LEACH	1950-1955
SCOTT MARSHALL	1951-1961
DAVID STANNARD	1952-1953
ROBIN WELCH	1953
DEREK EMMS	1954-1955
LEN CASTLE	1956-1957
ANNE KJAERSGAARD	1956-1958
PETER STICHBURY	1957
RICHARD BATTERHAM	1957-1958
ATSUYA HAMADA	1957-1958
HELENA KLUG	1958

GWYN HANSSEN-PIGOTT	1958-1959
JOHN REEVE	1958-1961 & 1966
MANSIMRAN SINGH	1959-1960
RICHARD JENKINS	1959-1961
BYRON TEMPLE	1959-1961 & 1978-1979
JOHN LEACH	1960-1963
NIRMALA PATWARDHAN	1961
GLENN LEWIS	1961-1963
SHINSAKU HAMADA	1963 Visitor
MIREK SMISEK	1963-1964
MICHAEL HENRY	1963-1965
JACK WORSELDINE	1963-1965
IAN STEEL	1963-1965 & 1967-1969
CLARY ILLIAN	1964-1965
TREVOR CORSER	1964-2005
ANTONY BURGESS	1965-1967
TIM STAMPTON	1965-1967
DENNY LONG	1966 Visitor
SYLVIA HARDAKER	1966-1968
CHANTAL DUNOYER	1967-1968
HARRY ISAACS	1967-1969
KENJI FUNAKI	1967 & 1975 Visitor
JOHN BEDDING	1968-1970 & 1972-1978
ALAN BROUGH	1968-1972
SHIGEYOSHI ICHINO	1969-1973
JEFF OESTREICH	1969-1971
PETER HARDY	1971-1973
MICHAEL CARTWRIGHT	1973-1975
IAN BOX	1974-1975
WILLIAM HENRY KLOCK	1975-1976
ROBERT FISHMAN	1976-1978
JEFFREY LARKIN	1976-1978
JASON WASON	1976-1981
NIC HARRISON	1979-1980
JOANNA WASON	1988-2005
TOMOO HAMADA	1995 Visitor
AMANDA BRIER	2000-2005

Potters with dates at Leach Pottery but not featured

TSURONOSUKE MATSUBAYASHI	1922-1924
SYLVIA FOX STRANGWAYS	1926
MURIEL BELL	1930-1931
KENNETH MURRAY	1935

HELEN PINCOMBE	1936
WILLIAM WORRELL	1937
JOHN BEW	1938
GEORGE WHITAKER	1938-1939
BARBARA MILLARD	1939
BUNTY SMITH	1940
PATRICK HERON (painter)	1944-1945
DICK KENDALL	1944-1946
GRATTAN FRYER	1945-1946
AILEEN NEWTON	1945-1946
ANNE-MARIE HARRISON	1948
ANNE MARIE BACKER-MOHR	1948-1950
WALTER GEORGE FIRTH	1948-1953
JUDY GARDNER	1952-1953
DINAH DUNN	1953-1958
PETER WOOD	1954-1955
ROBERT KING	1965-1967
SUSAN SMITH	1966-1967
WAYNE PINDER	1969-1971
BRENDA TINKLIN	1978-1980

Other potters without dates
PATRICIA ASHMORE
JOHN CONEY
MARCIA COX
PIERRE CULOT
BERYL DEBNEY
ELIZABETH HEINZ
JORGEN JORGENSEN
SUSAN KRAFT
PAUL LAJOIRE
RUTH LYLE
SUSAN MARSHALL
KIM PERRY
PETER SNAGG
MICHAEL TRUSCOTT
ZELIA VANDENBERG
SUSAN WOOD
ZADRE

Apologies to those Leach potters not identified despite the author's extensive research

Other Books by Marion Whybrow

Published Books

St Ives 1883-1993 : Portrait of an Art Colony

The Leach Legacy : St Ives Pottery and its Influence 1996

The Innocent Eye: Primitive & Naïve Painters in Cornwall

Bryan Pearce : A Private View

Virginia Woolf and Vanessa Bell : Remembering St Ives.

Co-author Marion Dell

Winner of a Holyer an Gof Gorseth Kernow Award

Smaller Books

Twenty Painters St Ives

Potters in their Place

Forms & Faces : Sculptors in the South West

Twenty Two Painters who Happen to be Women

Studio : Artists in their Workplace

Another View : Art in St Ives

Plays

O.A.P. Rules OK

Sweet Venom – Cornwall Drama Award (unpublished)

Novels

Shadow Over Summer

Gorsemoor Cottage

Narcissus Road (in creation)

Quotes

1 *The Potter's Challenge,* Bernard Leach, page 21, Souvenir Press 1976
2 *Beyond East and West,* Bernard Leach, page 156. Faber & Faber 1978
3 Warren MacKenzie. Letter to the author 1994
4 St Ives Times 1920
5 St Ives Times 1927
6 & 7 *A Pioneer Potter, an autobiography,* Michael Cardew, pages 26 and 39 Wm Collins 1988
8 & 9 *Beyond East & West,* Bernard Leach, page 216 & 217. Faber & Faber 1978
10 *The Changing Forms of Art,* Patrick Heron, page 57. Routledge & Kegan Paul 1955
11 Conversation with David Leach 1994
12 Catalogue of Leach Pottery 1954
13,14,15 Valerie Bond (Prescott) Letters to the author 1994
16 *Hamada Potter* by Bernard Leach, page 134. Thames & Hudson 1976
17 Janet Leach Journal of 1954
18 Janet Leach, *Fifty One Years of the Leach Pottery.* Ceramic Review, Issue 14 March/April 1972
18a Ibid
19 Janet Leach, *Tribute to Bernard Leach,* Ceramic Review No.58 July/August 1979
19a St Ives Times & Echo 28/7/2000
20 Leach Profile *What Can a Potter Say?* by Karin Fernald BBC
21 Newspaper article written in English by Oshiko Uchida, Japan 1954
22 Quote from Janet Leach 1995
23 *Hamada Potter* by Bernard Leach page 134. Thames & Hudson 1976
24 Ceramic Review March/April No.122, 1990, page 13
25 *Michael Cardew, A Pioneer Potter,* page 11. Wm Collins 1988
26 *Gutte Eriksen* by David Whiting. Studio Pottery No 16 Aug/Sept1995
27 *A Potter in Japan 1952-54* by Bernard Leach, page 93. Faber & Faber 1960
28 *Hamada Potter* by Bernard Leach, page 115. Thames & Hudson Ltd 1975
29, 30 *Katharine Pleydell-Bouverie, A Potter's Life 1895-1985,* Crafts Council 1986
31 *Beyond East and West* by Bernard Leach, page 259. Faber & Faber 1978
32, 33 Letter to Geoffrey Whiting from Bernard Leach 7/11/1955

Glossary of Terms

Ashes
The remains of trees, plants, bones used by the potter as a source of body and glaze fluxes.
Biscuit
First firing.
Body
The clay of which a pot is made.
Celadon
A grey-green to grey-blue stoneware and porcelain glaze.
Clay
Basic material refined and processed by the potter. (there are many types of clay)
Earthenware
Pottery made of a porous body which is waterproofed, if necessary, by a covering glaze.
Enamel
A soft-melting glass used to decorate pottery, metal and glass.
English slipware
Lead-glazed pottery, usually on a red body and decorated with slip by dipping, trailing and sgraffito.
Firing
The burning or stoking of a kiln. The process of conversion from clay to pot.
Glaze
A layer of glass which is fused into place on a pottery body.
Porcelain
Applies to pottery which is white, vitrified and translucent.
Raku
A Japanese method of firing pots at low temperature.
Slip
A mixture of clay and water used for coating clays.
Slipware
Earthenware pottery decorated with coloured slips under a transparent lead glaze.
Sgraffito
Scratched decoration on the body of a pot.
Stoneware
A hard, strong and vitrified pottery ware.
Tenmoku
A lustrous-black iron stoneware glaze.
Wedging
A process of preparing plastic clay which involves mixing and pressing the clay by hand to expel air.

Acknowledgements

Personal Acknowledgements
My husband, Terry Whybrow, for always being there.
My daughter, Kim Lynch, for her expertise in designing the book.
My five colleagues John Bedding, Jon Grimble, Denny Long, Trixie Lucas, Roger Tonkinson

Acknowledgements
With thanks to all the potters, and others, who provided information on pots and people.
Alan Gillam (Leach Pottery)
Andrew Marshall (Atsuya Hamada)
Daryl Fromm Collection (Bill Marshall, Richard Batterham)
Gill Groves (Leach Pottery)
Hardingham Collection, (Cecil Baugh)
Hyman Segal, drawing of Bernard Leach
Jeremy Quick for loaning pots of Margaret Leach, Kenneth Quick, Shoji Hamada.
John Bedding for various pots
Kim Lynch for cover design.
K Pleydell-Bouverie, John Reeve
Michelle Wright for French translations
Paul Vibert for loan of Bernard Leach drawing on title page
Roger Tonkinson (Harry Davis, Byron Temple) and collection of standard ware
Sachiko Quayle for identifying names of Mashiko delegation
Sayuri Lily Hill for Japanese translations
St Ives Trust & Archive Study Centre, St Andrew's Street, St Ives
Valerie Bond collection of photos
West Cornwall Art Archive, Trevelyan House, Penzance

Photo Credits

John Bedding, *photo of Leach standard ware on front cover and others*
Ben Boswell, *photo Janet Leach*
Ben Boswell, *photo Michael Cardew*
Bret Guthrie, *Bernard Leach loading kiln 1920*
Brian Hand, *Gwyn Hanssen Pigott pots*
Bylyne Image Management, *John Leach pots*
Ceramic Review, *some David Leach pots*
Cornelia Wingfield Digby, *permission to take photos St Ives Tate Collection*
Courtesy of Baugh: Jamaica's Master Potter. Miami DLT Associates Inc.1999
David Coleman, *John Reeve and pots*
David Lay, Auctioneer, *for photos of pots*
Denis Valentine, *Cecil Baugh pot*
Derek Emms, *various photos*
Doreen Bennett, *Sylvia Hardaker pots*
Duncan Painter, *Michael Cardew pot*
Geoff Meadowcroft, *Charlotte Epton pots*
Harry Isaacs, *Janet's kiln supper*
Henry Rothchild by kind permission *(Michael Cardew)*
Holburne Museum & Crafts Study Centre, Katharine Pleydell-Bouverie, *Norah Braden*
Howard Ursuliak, *Glenn Lewis pots*
Joanna Bird Collection *(Michael Cardew)*
John Bedding, *photo of Leach standard ware on front cover*
John Kostle, *Clary Ilian and pot*
Judith Davidoff (nee Perkins), *Denny Long*
Kenneth Quick collection
Leif Tuxan, *Gutte Eriksen*
Nigel Cheffers Heard, *Bernard Forrester*
Owen Minott, *Cecil Baugh*
Paul Vincent, *Michael Leach pot*
Peter Gilbert, *Harry Isaacs*
Peter Kinnear, *Janet Leach pots*
Phil Monkton, *David Leach, Marion Whybrow, Janet Leach, book signing Tate St Ives 1996*
Raymond Sauvaire, *Helena Klug and pots*
Robert Jewell, *Nic Harrison pots*
Ron Sloman, *John Leach pots*
Ron Sutherland, *Trevor Corser pots*
Seiji Okumiya, *Trevor Corser*
Simon Cook, *Denny Long pots*
Stephen Brayne, *Richard Batterham and William Marshall pots*
St Ives Times & Echo, *book launch at Tate St Ives 1994*
St Ives Times & Echo, *Mashiko delegation*
Tomoo Hamada, *permission to use family photos*
Torquil Macleod, *David Leach and Tomoo Hamada at Dartington 1995*

Bibliography

Barrow,T (1960) *Bernard Leach, Essays in Appreciation*, Wellington N Zealand

Batterham, Richard (1990) *Potter,* Ceramic Review 122

Birks, Tony and Cornelia Wingfield Digby (1990) Bernard Leach, *Hamada & Their Circle, from the Wingfield Digby Collection* Phaidon

Browning, Vivienne *St Ives Summer 1946 The Leach Pottery,* The Book Gallery 1995

Cardew, Michael (1969) *Pioneer Pottery,* Longmans

Cardew, Michael (1988) *A Pioneer Potter, An Autobiography*. Wm Collins

Carter, Pat (1990) *A Dictionary of British Studio Potters,* Scolar Press

Clark ,Garth (1978) Michael Cardew, *An Intimate Account of a Potter who has captured the spirit of country craft,* Faber & Faber

Clark, Garth *The Potter's Art,* (1995) Phaidon,

Cooper, Emmanuel (2003) *Bernard Leach Life and Work,* Yale University Press

Cooper, Emmanuel (2003) *David Leach A Biography,* Richard Dennis

Craft Potters Association (1994) *10th Edition illustrated directory of Fellows & Professional members,* Ceramic Review

Dartington Cider Press (1993) *Dartington 60 years of Pottery 1933-1993,*

Davis, Harry (1988) *The Complete Potter.* Ceramic Review

Davis, May (1990) *May, Her Story,* New Zealand

Fournier, Robert (1977) *David Leach, A Potter's Life*

Fournier, Robert and Sheila (1994) *A Guide to Public Collections of Studio Pottery in the British Isles,* Ceramic Review Publishing

Galerie Besson Catalogue (1995) *Gutte Eriksen*

Gaymard, Elisabeth (1985) *Anne Kjaersgaard,* La Revue de la Ceramique et du Verre

Hogben, Carol (1978) *The Art of Bernard Leach,* Faber & Faber

Kemp, Dorothy (1954) *English Slipware and How to Make it,* Faber & Faber

Lane, W H (1981) *Leach Bernard, Shoji Hamada* , Auction Catalogue, Penzance

Lay, David (1994) *British Studio Pottery,* Auction Catalogue, Penzance

Leach, Bernard (1928) *A Potter's Outlook*

Leach, Bernard (1940) *A Potter's Book,* Faber (and later editions)

Leach, Bernard (1946) *The Leach Pottery 1920-1946,* Berkley Galleries

Leach, Bernard (1948) *The Contemporary Studio-Potter,* Royal Society of Arts

Leach, Bernard (1951) *A Potter's Portfolio, A selection of fine pots,* Lund Humphries

Leach, Bernard (1952) *The Leach Pottery 1920-1952*

Leach, Bernard (1955) *Letter to Geoffrey Whiting,* 7 November 1955

Leach, Bernard (1960) *A Potter in Japan 1952-54,* Faber & Faber

Leach, Bernard (1966) Kenzan & his tradition. *The Lives & Times of Koetsu, Sotatsu, Korin & Kenzan,* Faber

Leach, Bernard (1968) *A compendium, compiled by St Ives Council , Honorary Freedom of the Borough to Bernard Leach & Barbara Hepworth*
Leach, Bernard (1973) *Drawings, Verse and Belief.* Jupiter Books
Leach, Bernard (1974) *A Potters' Work,* Adams & Dart
Leach, Bernard (1976) *Hamada, Potter,* Thames & Hudson
Leach, Bernard (1976) *The Potter's Challenge,* Souvenir Press
Leach, Bernard (1978) *Beyond East & West, Memoirs, Portraits & Essays,* Faber
Leach, Bernard (1980) *Ceramics Auction,* W H Lane, Penzance
Leach, Bernard (1992) *Hamada & Their Circle,* Wingfield Digby Collection
Leach, Janet *Going to Pot,* (1981) Ceramic Review No 71, Sept/Oct
Leach, Janet (1972) *Fifty One Years of the Leach Pottery,* Ceramic Review No 14
Lewis, David (1991) Warren MacKenzie, *An American Potter,* Kodansha International
Moncrieff, Elspeth (1995) *Norah Braden, A talent lain long dormant* (newspaper article unknown source)
Naylor, Barrie *Quakers in the Rhondda*
Pleydell-Bouverie, Katharine (1986) *A Potter's Life,* Crafts Council
Rice, Paul and Christopher Gowing (1989) *British Studio Ceramics in the 20th Century,* Barrie and Jenkins, London
Rose, Muriel (1970) *Artist Potters in England,* Faber & Faber
Studio Pottery, Feb/Mar 1994, Edited by Paul Vincent
Tanna, Laura and Baugh, Cecil (1999) *Jamaica's Master Potter*
Uchida, Oshiko (1954) *Newspaper article written in English* (Hamada profile) Japan
Victoria and Albert Museum (1977) *The Art of Bernard Leach*
Watson, Oliver (1993) *Studio Pottery,* Phaidon
Wheeler, Ron (1998) *Winchcombe Pottery, The Cardew, Finch Tradition*
Whiting, David (1994) Geoffrey *Whiting 1919-1988,* Studio Pottery No.11 Oct/Nov
Whiting, David (1995) *Gutte Eriksen,* Studio Pottery No.16 Aug/Sept
Whybrow, Marion (1994) *St Ives 1883-1993 Portrait of an Art Colony,* Antique Collectors' Club. Reprint Harbour Bookshop, St Ives
Whybrow, Marion (1996) *The Leach Legacy - St Ives Pottery and its Influence* Sansom & Company, Bristol
Yanagi, Soetsu (1972 & 1989) *The Unknown Craftsman. A Japanese insight into Beauty.* Iokyo, Kadansha International

Films and Tapes

The Art of the Potter, East/West Productions 331 West 11th Street, New York, NY 10014 - 50 minute film of the process of pottery making filmed in Mashiko, Japan with Hamada and interview with Bernard Leach (no date)

Fernald, Karin *What Can A Potter Say?* BBC (no date)

The Leach Pottery 1952 film of Bernard Leach, David Leach, Kenneth Quick and others making pots, with no commentary.

A Potter's World, BBC film of St Ives Pottery, 1960

N.H.K. Television film of Bernard Leach, 1974

Ismay, W A (1977) David Leach, A Monograph. Tapes by Bernard and David Leach

Leach, David (1990) Pots, Boston Radio Interview with Dick Pleasant

Leach, David (1989) The Leach Influence, Bristol Poly

The Stories of Two Great South West Artists, Leach and Hepworth, Television South West. Video taken from earlier films 1995

Archive Film of Bernard Leach 1952

Index

Page numbers in bold refer to illustrations.